# Cleveland Indians IQ: The Ultimate Test of True Fandom

TUCKER ELLIOT
DERRYL WALDEN

Cataloging-in-Publication Data is available from the Library of Congress.
ISBN: 978-0-9883648-3-7
First edition, first printing.

Cover photo courtesy of Mark Whitt.
Cover design by Holly Walden Ross.

Black Mesa Publishing, LLC
Florida

Black.Mesa.Publishing@gmail.com
www.blackmesabooks.com

# Cleveland Indians

# CONTENTS

*"There are only two seasons—winter and baseball."*
— Bill Veeck, Hall of Fame executive

# INTRODUCTION

I **GREW UP** around baseball. Outside and barefoot is the way I describe spending my childhood. I grew up with two brothers, and in the middle of Nowhere, Florida there was not much else to distract us—so we played, relentlessly. And while my mom had to drive an hour one way to find a shopping mall, every March we'd drive slightly more than that and find ourselves at any number of Spring Training sites. We'd watch games in Tampa, Plant City, Lakeland, Vero Beach, Fort Myers … too many places to remember, actually. And in the summer we'd drive to Atlanta to see big league action in the regular season. Once we even drove to Arlington, Texas. It took two days to get there, but attending a Rangers vs. Red Sox Monday Night Baseball Game of the Week was worth it.

There was no shortage of baseball in my childhood.

We'd play ball in the spring, summer, and fall—and we'd practice in the winter. And as a kid, I must have assumed that my dad's childhood was spent in much the same way. After all, my dad was always scouring yard sales and flea markets for old baseball cards, often paying a buck or less for a shoebox full of amazing treasures, and then bringing them home and laughing with pure joy as he saw the excitement on our faces. And he was always outside with us, throwing BP or playing catch or hitting grounders. We'd been at this for a lot of years before I found out that my dad's childhood was nothing at all like mine, that the memories he was helping us make as kids were also helping to fill the void in his own mind. My dad did play sports in high school, of course—and he was good, too. He starred in basketball and as the quarterback for his high school football team. But the part missing from his childhood was being able to share something like a simple game of catch with your dad. And that's what he worked so hard to give us.

He also worked hard to keep some things from us. Vietnam, for example, or earlier, attending nearly a dozen different schools in the span of two years after his parents divorced. There were certain hardships, certain ugly realities about life that he felt compelled to protect us from, even if they were far in the distant past and couldn't reach out to hurt us. As we grew older, it was easier to understand that some things just weren't to be talked about—and while we all respected that, as a young kid not yet in middle school, I was already in love with stories and writing and history, and my relentless pursuit of baseball was not limited to sandlot games or shoeboxes full of baseball cards. I heard story after story about the Yankees and Red Sox from my grandfather (my mom's dad), I heard stories about the Indians from my mom's brother, who when he was a kid was probably the only Indians fan in South Carolina, and I pressed my dad for him to tell me stories, too. And he did, but there was a pattern to them. He'd tell me about Sandy Koufax throwing a no-hitter, for example. But that's no different than me telling my nephew today about Kirk Gibson's home run in the 1988 World Series. I was a kid watching it on TV, but I wasn't there. It's still a great story, but what I wanted from my dad was something real—I wanted something that he experienced.

And then one day my dad disappeared into the back of the house and I heard him rummaging through a closet. He returned with a small box that held old black and white photographs, newspaper clippings, a business card from a tailor shop in Hong Kong (R&R from Vietnam, I later learned), a Tiger patch that was the designation for a Korean army unit that served alongside him and that was given to him by a friend he'd never told me about until that day, and I'm sure a few other items I can't remember, but also one more item that I'll never forget: a ticket stub. And then my dad told me the greatest baseball story I'd ever heard.

It was 1963 and my dad had been out of high school for a few months and taking a few classes in college. But he was young and independent and looking for something better than what he'd been dealt so far in life. He needed a job to earn and save for college, and I'm sure jobs were available in Gainesville where he was living, but he also needed movement, as in, just don't stand still. He needed to believe his life was going forward, going places more promising than where he'd been already. And so, just because they could, he and a childhood friend named Jimmy Weber packed a couple of bags and drove north looking for work in a 1950s VW beetle. In Columbia, they stopped and slept on the football field at the University of South

Carolina—because they could, and besides, it was cheaper than a hotel. They ended up in Virginia Beach, VA, serving ice cream and grilling hamburgers and hot dogs and saving a little bit of money. After two months, the summer was getting short and soon it'd be time to return to Florida and his life, as he'd known it before.

But Jimmy had family in Michigan. And they had a house on a lake, and that sounded about perfect to my dad, who was willing to go anywhere as long as he kept moving forward, who was willing to do anything to not stand still, to not live in the past. So willing, that he'd later go to Vietnam to pay for college—to just move forward. So they left Virginia for Michigan, and along the way they stopped for the night in Cleveland. My dad was thumbing through a paper, looking at the sports section, and realized the Indians were playing a doubleheader against the Los Angeles Angels the following day.

He'd never been to a big league game before.

It was July 31, 1963, and my dad felt like a kid walking through the turnstiles at Cleveland Stadium. The stadium was largely empty, with just over 7,000 fans in attendance. It didn't matter to my dad, the whole atmosphere was surreal, and he loved it. The Indians won the first game in a pitcher's duel, 1-0. That's a pretty rare score, and my dad was impressed that his first big league game had ended that way. He was excited to see what was in store for him in the second game, and it didn't disappoint. Cleveland won 9-5, but it wasn't the score that people would remember or talk about, it was a piece of history that took place in the home half of the sixth inning: Woodie Held, Pedro Ramos, Tito Francona, and Larry Brown connected on four consecutive home runs.

There'd been a home run earlier in the game, and my dad had been thrilled to see one in person.

But in the sixth, when Ramos connected for back-to-back jacks he was ecstatic. He was thinking this day couldn't get any better. And then Francona went yard. Three in a row. And then the crowd was going crazy. It was like the baseball gods were showing off just for him, in honor of his first day of big league baseball. And surely the baseball gods were smiling that day, because the next batter was Larry Brown, and he was a scrawny, scrappy 23-year-old kid who'd never hit a big league home run. And yet he stepped to the plate and became just the second player in baseball history to connect and give his team four consecutive home runs.

My dad laughed as he told me the story. He said the PA announcer told the crowd they'd just witnessed a Major League record. And then my dad checked to make sure he still had his ticket stub in his pocket, and he made sure he saved it—but not really because of the record, he saved it because of the day, because of the experience, because it was his first time sitting in the stands watching Major League baseball, and he was sure he never wanted to forget it.

I was in awe, and later I was jealous. I'd been to hundreds of games and never witnessed anything close to what my dad had seen on that one day.

I don't know how long we talked about that game the first time my dad showed me the ticket stub. He admitted he hadn't even been sure that he still had it, that he was surprised when he'd been able to find it. But we've spent hours and hours and hours talking about it since. And it's pretty amazing, because that ticket stub sat in a box for two decades—once it let my dad into a stadium to see a baseball game, and then later, it let me into my dad's world, into his past, to learn about the man who taught me to love a game so passionately that it shaped nearly every aspect of my life.

I have my dad's ticket stub today. It's on my wall, in a frame, along with the newspaper clipping from that historic game. I've still never witnessed anything like it, but that's OK, because I still go to games with my dad and mom, and my brothers, and my nieces and nephews. And my dad's story gave me a new team to root for, and I've really no idea how it works that way, only that it does. Because when I found out what that one Indians game had meant to my dad, somehow I felt I owed the Indians something in return. The first time I saw the Indians play in person was Game 1 of the 1995 World Series. I grew up a diehard Braves fan, but I remember sitting above third base at Fulton County Stadium and thinking this was just about perfect because no matter what happened there was something I was going to be thankful for—I'd played high school baseball against Chipper Jones and wanted to see him win, my uncle had been rooting for the Indians since the 1950s and wanted to see Cleveland win, and then I had my dad's story, of course. And it was perfect, because it was baseball.

I've written or contributed to more than 40 books now—one of my first was on the Braves, and I've wanted and planned to write about the Indians for years. Every time I'd sit at my desk to write, I'd see that ticket stub and wonder why I was writing again about the Yankees or Red Sox. Well, I'm glad I finally wrote about Cleveland, its rich history and traditions, and the many great players and moments that have inspired generations of fans. And I hope these pages let you recall some great memories from your own past and the people you shared them with.

*Tucker Elliot*
*August 2012*
*Tampa FL*

*"I would rather beat the Yankees regularly than pitch a no-hit game."*
— Bob Feller, Hall of Fame legend

# 1 THE NUMBERS GAME

**THE CLEVELAND INDIANS** Hall of Fame currently has 46 members—including Gaylord Perry, Jim Warfield, and Jack Graney who were inducted in August 2012. Among the many great names already enshrined are Sandy Alomar Jr., Kenny Lofton, Lou Boudreau, Stan Coveleski, Rocky Colavito, Larry Doby, Bob Feller, Mike Hargrove, Bob Lemon, Herb Score, Joe Sewell, Tris Speaker, and Early Wynn. It's a select group, for sure.

And you'll find all those names in this book.

To start off, though, we look at 20 of the many great players who suited it up for the Indians—six who had their jersey numbers retired by the club, followed by 14 others who demonstrated monstrous power, lightning speed, slick fielding ability, or an incredible mound presence—and then challenge you to a simple numbers game. Can you recall what jersey number each of these stars wore for the Indians?

Let's find out.

**QUESTION 1:** Earl Averill played 11 of his 13 Major League seasons with the Indians. A .318 career hitter, the Hall of Fame legend and six-time All-Star retired as the franchise leader in runs (1,154), triples (121), home runs (226), and extra-base hits (724). Averill, who batted lefty, spoke about his approach to hitting, saying, "I kept two things in mind at the plate—one was that I was up there to swing, and the other was to keep my eye on my target. That was the pitcher's cap. I always aimed for that, tried to go to the middle. But, if the ball was outside, I'd hit to left." Averill wore four different jersey numbers in his career—3, 5, 24, and 27. Which one of these jersey numbers did the Indians retire in his honor?

    a)   3
    b)   5

c)   24
d)   27

**QUESTION 2:** Lou Boudreau played 13 of his 15 Major League seasons with the Indians. The Hall of Fame shortstop was a seven-time All-Star with the Indians and was known throughout his career for being a defensive genius. And he could hit, too. Boudreau led the league in doubles three times and batted .295 for his career. What jersey number did the Indians retire in his honor?

a)   3
b)   5
c)   23
d)   31

**QUESTION 3:** Larry Doby played ten of his 13 Major League seasons with the Indians. The Hall of Fame legend was an All-Star in seven consecutive seasons from 1949-55 and was a two-time home run champion. What jersey number did the Indians retire in his honor?

a)   6
b)   14
c)   32
d)   37

**QUESTION 4:** Mel Harder spent parts of 20 seasons as a Major League pitcher—every one of them with the Indians, making him the longest tenured player in franchise history. He was a four-time All-Star and 14 times he had double-digits in victories. What jersey number did the Indians retire in his honor?

a)   18
b)   27
c)   39
d)   49

**QUESTION 5:** Bob Feller played every one of his 18 Major League seasons with the Indians. The Hall of Fame legend is the franchise leader in wins and strikeouts—and he led the league in strikeouts seven times. Ted Lyons once said, "It wasn't until you hit against him [Feller] that you knew how fast he really was, until you saw with your own eyes that ball jumping at you." What jersey number did the Indians retire in his honor?

a)   9
b)   14
c)   19
d)   29

**QUESTION 6:** Bob Lemon played every one of his 13 Major League seasons with the Indians. The Hall of Famer was a seven-time All-Star who led the league in wins three times, and he is also one of just four American League pitchers to win 20 or more games in seven different seasons. What jersey number did the Indians retire in his honor?

a)   6
b)   21
c)   38
d)   42

**QUESTION 7:** Jim Thome was a 20-year-old prospect when he made his big league debut with the Indians in 1991. He hit one home run in 27 games that season. Thome, of course, is one of baseball's all-time greatest sluggers. He spent his first 12 big league seasons with the Indians, and nearly a decade after leaving for Philly, he rejoined the club during the stretch run at the end of 2011. What was Thome's primary jersey number with the Indians?

a)   6
b)   19
c)   25
d)   59

**QUESTION 8:** Manny Ramirez was a 21-year-old prospect when he made his big league debut with the Indians in 1993. He hit two home runs in 22 games that season. And like Thome, he became one of the game's greatest sluggers during his eight years with the Tribe. What was Ramirez's primary jersey number with the Indians?

a)   8
b)   24
c)   31
d)   39

**QUESTION 9:** Albert Belle was one of the game's most feared sluggers during his eight seasons with the Indians. A prolific home run hitter and consistent run producer, he burst onto the scene in 1991 and abused American League pitching for the rest of the decade. What was Belle's primary jersey number with the Indians?

    a)   8
    b)   23
    c)   36
    d)   88

**QUESTION 10:** Travis Hafner made his big league debut for the Texas Rangers in 2002. He hit one home run in 23 games that season and then he was traded to the Indians. He's been slowed by injuries in recent years, but from 2003-07 his powerful bat gave many sleepless nights to opposing pitchers. What was Hafner's primary jersey number with the Indians during that time?

    a)   6
    b)   32
    c)   48
    d)   51

**QUESTION 11:** Kenny Lofton had two steals in 20 games with the Astros during a September 1991 call-up—his first taste of Major League action. He was traded in the offseason to the Indians and had an immediate impact. Lofton led the American League in steals five consecutive seasons from 1992-96. What was Lofton's primary jersey number during his first tenure with the Indians?

    a)   1
    b)   7
    c)   12
    d)   28

**QUESTION 12:** Buddy Bell was a slick fielder who made his first All-Star team as a 21-year-old third baseman with the Indians in 1973. Bell played seven seasons with the Tribe until he was traded to the Texas Rangers for Toby Harrah in December 1978. So of course in 1979, Bell had the finest offensive season of his career and won the first of six consecutive Gold Glove Awards. He was a five-time All-

Star for his career—once with the Indians and four times with the Rangers. What was Bell's primary jersey number with the Indians?

a) 9
b) 19
c) 25
d) 29

**QUESTION 13:** Joe Carter was the second overall pick in the 1981 draft by the Chicago Cubs and he made his big league debut in 1983. He came to the Indians as part of the trade that sent Rick Sutcliffe to the Cubs in June 1984. A week later he made his American League debut, three days after that he hit his first big league home run, and he finished the season batting .275 with 13 homers and 41 RBIs in only 66 games. What was Carter's primary jersey number with the Indians?

a) 17
b) 29
c) 30
d) 43

**QUESTION 14:** The Seattle Mariners traded Omar Vizquel to Cleveland in December 1993. The shortstop was a three-time All-Star and won eight Gold Gloves during 11 seasons with the Tribe. What was Vizquel's primary jersey number with the Indians?

a) 13
b) 19
c) 23
d) 42

**QUESTION 15:** Cory Snyder was the fourth overall pick in the first round of the 1984 draft by the Cleveland Indians. He also starred on the U.S. Olympic team in 1984. Snyder made his big league debut with the Tribe in 1986 and hit 24 home runs in only 103 games. What was Snyder's primary jersey number with the Indians?

a) 17
b) 18
c) 27
d) 28

**QUESTION 16:** In January 2012, the Indians announced that Gaylord Perry would be inducted into the team's Hall of Fame during a pregame ceremony on August 11, 2012. Perry spent three-plus seasons with the Tribe from 1972-75, and in that time he was an All-Star twice and he compiled a 70-57 record with a 2.51 earned run average. Perry wore No. 35 on his jersey in 1972, but what was the primary jersey number he wore during the rest of his tenure with the Indians?

    a)   22
    b)   28
    c)   36
    d)   46

**QUESTION 17:** Early Wynn is one of only two players in Major League history to finish his career with exactly 300 wins (the other is Lefty Grove). The Hall of Fame legend played ten years and won 164 of those games in Cleveland. A fierce competitor, Wynn once said, "A pitcher has to look at the hitter as his mortal enemy." His stats suggest he prevailed against his enemies more times than not. What was Wynn's primary jersey number with the Indians?

    a)   11
    b)   24
    c)   38
    d)   44

**QUESTION 18:** Charles Nagy was inducted into the Cleveland Indians Hall of Fame in August 2007. The pitcher was a three-time All-Star and he won 15-plus games six times for the club, including five consecutive seasons from 1995-99. Nagy said this of his selection: "I'm very aware of the organization's rich history, which makes this honor so very special to me and my family … I immediately thought of how fortunate I was to play alongside great teammates and in front of such passionate baseball fans." What was Nagy's primary jersey number with the Indians?

    a)   29
    b)   31
    c)   39
    d)   41

**QUESTION 19:** Andre Thornton hit 214 home runs during ten seasons with the Indians. The powerful first baseman / DH was inducted into the Indians Hall of Fame alongside Charles Nagy in 2007. Thornton said, "Being named to the Indians Hall of Fame means a great deal to me. It is an incredible honor to be a player that performed well enough to be selected as a member to join such an elite group." What was Thornton's primary jersey number with the Indians?

    a)   29
    b)   34
    c)   39
    d)   44

**QUESTION 20:** Sandy Alomar Jr. was one of the Tribe's most popular players. He spent 11 seasons with the club and was a six-time All-Star. Alomar was inducted into the Indians Hall of Fame in 2009, and later that year he joined the Indians coaching staff. What was Alomar's primary jersey number with the Indians?

    a)   4
    b)   15
    c)   17
    d)   25

# 1 ANSWER KEY

| | |
|---|---|
| ___ **QUESTION 1:** A | ___ **QUESTION 11:** B |
| ___ **QUESTION 2:** B | ___ **QUESTION 12:** C |
| ___ **QUESTION 3:** B | ___ **QUESTION 13:** C |
| ___ **QUESTION 4:** A | ___ **QUESTION 14:** A |
| ___ **QUESTION 5:** C | ___ **QUESTION 15:** D |
| ___ **QUESTION 6:** B | ___ **QUESTION 16:** C |
| ___ **QUESTION 7:** C | ___ **QUESTION 17:** B |
| ___ **QUESTION 8:** B | ___ **QUESTION 18:** D |
| ___ **QUESTION 9:** A | ___ **QUESTION 19:** A |
| ___ **QUESTION 10:** C | ___ **QUESTION 20:** B |

**KEEP A RUNNING TALLY OF YOUR CORRECT ANSWERS!**

Number correct:   ___ / 20

Overall correct:   ___ / 20

*"It's the biggest thrill of my life. I'm deeply honored."*
— Herb Score, after winning 1955 Rookie of the Year honors

# 2 THE ROOKIES

**THE CLEVELAND INDIANS** first Rookie of the Year recipient was Herb Score. The lefty threw bullets at hitters and established a Major League rookie record in 1955—and that record is the subject of our first question in this chapter on Cleveland's great rookies.

The 1971 American League Rookie of the Year also played for the Indians—and he had a cousin who starred for the Boston Celtics at that same time. Joe Charboneau (1980) and Sandy Alomar Jr. (1990) also won the award for the Indians. You'll find all the Indians rookie award winners in this chapter, along with some astounding rookie performances like CC Sabathia winning 13 games on the road in 2001 and Kenny Lofton's league leading 66 steals in 1992. How much do you know about Cleveland's greatest rookies?

Let's find out.

**QUESTION 21:** Herb Score was the 1955 American League Rookie of the Year after posting a 16-10 record with a 2.85 earned run average. The hard throwing lefty gave up just 158 hits in 227 innings of work. Rocky Colavito said of Score, "They didn't have a radar gun then to measure speed but I think he threw 100 miles an hour." Score also set a Major League record for rookies that lasted nearly three decades. What rookie record did Score set in 1955?

    a)   2.85 ERA
    b)   9.7 strikeouts per nine innings
    c)   245 strikeouts
    d)   11 complete games

**QUESTION 22:** Jo Jo White was a first round draft pick of the Boston Celtics out of the University of Kansas in 1969, and he made the NBA's All-Rookie 1st Team in 1969-70. White would later win the NBA Finals MVP Award in 1975-76. Oddly enough, White's cousin was the number one overall pick out of UCLA by the

Cleveland Indians during the 1970 draft, one year later he was the American League Rookie of the Year, and in the same season that White was the NBA Finals MVP, his cousin hit a home run to win the American League Pennant for the Yankees. Who is Jo Jo White's cousin?

    a)   Ted Ford
    b)   Chris Chambliss
    c)   Jim Clark
    d)   Buddy Bradford

**QUESTION 23:** Joe Charboneau made his big league debut on April 11, 1980, batting seventh and playing left field for the Indians vs. the Angels. In the top of the fifth, in his second career at bat, he blasted a long home run to right centerfield against Angels pitcher Dave Frost. It was a great start to his rookie season, and he had more memorable moments in store. In July, Charboneau had a stretch in which he hit three home runs and had 14 RBIs in five games. In August, he had a stretch in which he hit four home runs with 11 RBIs in seven games. All total, he batted .289 with 23 home runs and 87 RBIs to claim Rookie of the Year honors. Unfortunately, his success was short-lived. Including the 23 home runs he hit as a rookie, how many career home runs did Joe Charboneau hit?

    a)   23
    b)   29
    c)   33
    d)   39

**QUESTION 24:** Sandy Alomar Jr. made his big league debut with the San Diego Padres on September 30, 1988. He got one at bat and he struck out. He played in seven games with the Padres in 1989 before joining the Indians for his full-fledged rookie season in 1990 (he came over in the trade that sent Joe Carter to San Diego). Alomar was an immediate hit in Cleveland. He batted .290 with nine home runs and 66 RBIs during 132 games catching for the Tribe. He was the unanimous Rookie of the Year recipient, handily beating out guys like Kevin Maas, John Olerud, and Robin Ventura, but that wasn't the only hardware Alomar won as a rookie. Which other award did Alomar win for the only time in his career during his 1990 rookie season?

a) Silver Slugger
b) Gold Glove
c) All-Star MVP
d) *Sporting News* Player of the Year

**QUESTION 25:** Jody Gerut was named *The Sporting News* AL Rookie of the Year in 2003, despite placing fourth in Rookie of the Year balloting behind Angel Berroa, Hideki Matsui, and Rocco Baldelli. Gerut batted .279 and led the Indians with 22 home runs and 75 RBIs in only 127 games. Unfortunately, he was bit hard by the injury bug prior to his sophomore season and never regained the same form he had as a rookie. Who was the last player before Gerut to lead the Indians in both home runs and RBIs during his rookie season?
a) Joe Charboneau, 1980
b) Joe Carter, 1984
c) Brook Jacoby, 1984
d) Cory Snyder, 1986

**QUESTION 26:** This Cleveland rookie made his debut on April 7, 1970, batting third and playing outfield vs. a strong Earl Weaver managed Baltimore Orioles club. He had two of the Indians measly four hits on the day, and he also drove in the Indians only two runs with a two-run home run in his second big league at bat. The Indians lost 8-2, but this player got his career off to a quick start—and then he built on that success to bat .268 with 23 home runs and 60 RBIs on the season. His strong showing earned him a second place finish in Rookie of the Year balloting behind the Yankees Thurman Munson. Who was this rookie?
a) Ray Fosse
b) Eddie Leon
c) Roy Foster
d) Graig Nettles

**QUESTION 27:** CC Sabathia was a 20-year-old rookie when he posted an impressive 17-5 record with the 2001 Indians. Sabathia was 7-3 during the season's first half, but after the break he caught fire—he was 10-2 down the stretch. He was also an astounding 13-2 on the road that season. He was Cleveland's first round pick and the 20th overall selection in the 1998 draft, and just three years later he was ...

runner-up in the American League Rookie of the Year balloting? That's right. Sabathia had an extraordinary year—probably one of the best ever by a player who did not win the league's top rookie honors. So ... who beat Sabathia to claim the award that season?

a) Ichiro Suzuki
b) Alfonso Soriano
c) Eric Hinske
d) Kazuhiro Sasaki

**QUESTION 28:** This slugger would almost certainly have won 2004 Rookie of the Year honors for the Indians ... if he'd still been a rookie. He'd played too many games during call-ups in 2002-03 to qualify as a rookie in 2004, despite the fact 2004 was his first full season with the club. And all he did was bat .283 with 23 home runs and 108 RBIs ... which got him a Silver Slugger and an All-Star nod, and that's not too shabby at all. Who is this slugger?

a) Travis Hafner
b) Grady Sizemore
c) Ben Broussard
d) Victor Martinez

**QUESTION 29:** The Cleveland Indians selected him out of Brigham Young and he rose through the ranks quickly, debuting with the Indians on June 13, 1986. Despite the late start to his rookie season he still hit 24 home runs and placed fourth in Rookie of the Year balloting behind the likes of Jose Canseco and Wally Joyner. Who is this slugger?

a) Mel Hall
b) Cory Snyder
c) Brook Jacoby
d) Dave Clark

**QUESTION 30:** This pitcher was the tenth overall pick in the first round of the 1994 draft by the Indians. He made his debut on June 24, 1997, as the Indians were in the midst of a race for the Division Title. He was 8-3 with a respectable 4.38 earned run average, placing a distant fifth in Rookie of the Year balloting. But what he did during the regular season is only part of the story. In the 1997 postseason the 21-year-old rookie was 2-0 vs. the Yankees in the Division Series and 3-0 for the playoffs, adding another win in the World Series vs. the Florida Marlins. He won Game 4 of the World Series and was in line to be the winning pitcher in Game 7 until the Marlins rallied late against the bullpen. Who is this pitcher?

a)  Paul Shuey
b)  Bartolo Colon
c)  Jaret Wright
d)  Brian Anderson

QUESTION 31: Manny Ramirez was the 13th overall pick in the first round of the 1991 draft by the Indians. That was the year the Yankees drafted lefty Brien Taylor out of high school with the first overall pick and signed him for $1.55 million ... only Taylor never made it to the majors. Taylor was released by the Yankees in 1998 and tried to latch on with the Mariners and Indians before retiring in 2000, making him just the second No. 1 pick in history to never make it to the big leagues. As for Manny, well ... by the time Taylor's career ended, Manny had already hit 236 big league home runs for the Indians—nearly as many as the six position players drafted ahead of him hit combined during their Major League careers. Manny's rookie season was 1994. He hit .269 with 17 home runs and 60 RBIs, and placed second in Rookie of the Year balloting. Who beat out Manny to win top rookie honors in 1994?

a)  Jim Edmonds
b)  Jeffrey Hammonds
c)  Bob Hamelin
d)  Jose Valentin

QUESTION 32: Kenny Lofton led the league with 66 steals during his 1992 rookie season. In 148 games, Lofton also scored 96 runs, batted .285, and he struck out just 54 times while drawing 68 walks. Lofton was second in Rookie of the Year balloting. The player who won the award stole 54 bases, scored 93 runs, and batted .290, but he struck out 124 times as opposed to drawing just 55 walks—and he was also caught stealing 18 times, second most in the league. Who beat out Kenny Lofton to win Rookie of the Year honors in 1992?

a)  Pat Listach
b)  Brady Anderson

c)   Luis Polonia
d)   Lance Johnson

**QUESTION 33:** Julio Franco made his big league debut in 1982, but he played in just 16 games and in the offseason was traded to the Indians. In 1983, Franco's first year with the Tribe and his official rookie season, he played shortstop and batted .273 with eight home runs and 80 RBIs. Franco placed second in Rookie of the Year balloting behind Ron Kittle, who hit 35 home runs with 100 RBIs for the White Sox. What team traded Franco to the Indians prior to his rookie season?

a)   Texas Rangers
b)   Chicago White Sox
c)   Philadelphia Phillies
d)   Milwaukee Brewers

**QUESTION 34:** This rookie was 20-7 and led the league with a 2.43 earned run average in 1948, placing second in Major League Rookie of the Year balloting. Even better, his 20th win came vs. the Boston Red Sox in the one-game playoff for the American League Pennant. Al Dark won Major League Rookie of the Year honors for the Boston Braves, but this pitcher tossed a complete game shutout against Dark and the Braves to win Game 3 of the World Series, and then he recorded five outs in scoreless relief to save the title-clinching Game 6. Who had this incredible rookie season for the 1948 Indians?

a)   Sam Zoldak
b)   Gene Bearden
c)   Bob Muncrief
d)   Don Black

**QUESTION 35:** This Hall of Fame pitcher began his career with Cleveland, posting a 13-7 record with a 2.60 earned run average during his rookie season. In total he was 40-32 during three seasons with the Tribe. Who is this legendary pitcher?

a)   Bert Blyleven
b)   Dennis Eckersley
c)   Gaylord Perry
d)   Stan Coveleski

**QUESTION 36:** Satchel Paige played in the Negro Leagues for the majority of his career. It wasn't until 1948 that he debuted in a Major League game. He was 6-1 with a 2.48 earned run average that season for the Indians. How old was the legendary Hall of Famer when he debuted in his 1948 "rookie" season?

a) 38
b) 40
c) 42
d) 44

**QUESTION 37:** The Indians were a miserable 57-105 in 1991. One of the few bright spots came on October 4, when this rookie hit the first home run of his Major League career. The Yankees were almost as bad that season, so it was hardly an important game—but it was still a dramatic moment for this 21-year-old slugger, who belted a long home run with two outs in the top of the ninth inning, on a 1-2 pitch no less. It proved to be the game-winner, as the Indians held on for a 2-1 victory. Who hit a game-winning blast for his first big league home run?

a) Mark Whiten
b) Chris James
c) Jim Thome
d) Carlos Baerga

**QUESTION 38:** This player was named the top prospect in the Indians organization by *Baseball America* in 2010. He made his big league debut that same year. After going hitless in his first game, he banged out a two-run double and a solo home run in his second big league game—and after nine games with the Indians he was batting .393 with five doubles and two homers. He suffered a season-ending injury in a collision at home plate after 46 games, but in that time he proved he deserved the high praise from *Baseball America*. Who made his big league debut to such high acclaim in 2010?

a) Michael Brantley
b) Luis Valbuena
c) Carlos Santana
d) Trevor Crowe

**QUESTION 39:** This Cleveland rookie led the league with 37 home runs in 1950. He'd played a total of 35 games without a Major League home run during call-ups from 1947-49, but in 1950 he batted .287 with 37 bombs, 116 RBIs, and 100 runs. He also set a franchise record for rookies when he homered in four consecutive games. Who posted these monstrous numbers during his 1950 rookie season?

a) Ray Boone
b) Bobby Avila
c) Jim Lemon
d) Al Rosen

**QUESTION 40:** It took 61 years for another Cleveland rookie to homer in four consecutive games. This player did it in 2011, and he was the first player in Major League history to do it within two weeks of making his debut, and just the second player in history to do it within his first ten games. Who got his career off to such a hot start in 2011?

a) Ezequiel Carrera
b) Lonnie Chisenhall
c) Jason Kipnis
d) Cord Phelps

## 2 ANSWER KEY

| | | | |
|---|---|---|---|
| ___ **QUESTION 21:** C* | | ___ **QUESTION 31:** C* |
| ___ **QUESTION 22:** B | | ___ **QUESTION 32:** A* |
| ___ **QUESTION 23:** B* | | ___ **QUESTION 33:** C |
| ___ **QUESTION 24:** B | | ___ **QUESTION 34:** B |
| ___ **QUESTION 25:** A | | ___ **QUESTION 35:** B |
| ___ **QUESTION 26:** C* | | ___ **QUESTION 36:** C |
| ___ **QUESTION 27:** A | | ___ **QUESTION 37:** C |
| ___ **QUESTION 28:** D | | ___ **QUESTION 38:** C |
| ___ **QUESTION 29:** B | | ___ **QUESTION 39:** D |
| ___ **QUESTION 30:** C | | ___ **QUESTION 40:** C |

**KEEP A RUNNING TALLY OF YOUR CORRECT ANSWERS!**

Number correct:    ___ / 20

Overall correct:    ___ / 40

#21 – The last rookie with 200 strikeouts was Grover Cleveland Alexander in 1911—but Alexander pitched 367 innings and had only 227 Ks; Dwight Gooden set the new ML record for rookies with 276 strikeouts in 1984.

#23 – He batted .210 with four home runs in 1981, and .214 with two home runs in 1982 before he was released.

#26 – Despite losing the AL Rookie of the Year, Foster was named *The Sporting News* Rookie of the Year—unfortunately, injuries soon followed and three years later he was out of the game.

#31 – Hamelin hit 24 home runs as a rookie—but finished his career with just 67 in parts of six big league seasons.

#32 – He stole just 116 bases in his career—Lofton stole 622.

*"He was a great American—he served the country in World War II and was a great ballplayer. He was kind of like Buzz Aldrin, the second man on the moon, because he was the second African American player in the Majors."*
— Bob Feller, on his teammate and Hall of Fame legend Larry Doby

# 3 THE VETERANS

THE INDIANS FRANCHISE is more than a century old. It's been called the Blues, the Bronchos, and the Naps. It's also been called a lot worse during hard times when the team wasn't winning. In its first 112 seasons, however, some of the most colorful and talented players in baseball history have called the Indians their home team. This chapter is about a select group of those players who provided a veteran presence in the Indians clubhouse.

Names like Thornton, Alomar, Thome, Hafner, Jacoby, Doby, Lemon, Feller, Boudreau and Carter ... and many more. All leaders in the clubhouse and on the field—and all with the ability to contribute to the team's success by virtue of hard won experience that defines the nature of a veteran player. But it would be a mistake to assume that because a player is a veteran that his contributions are limited to "experience." Talent plus hard work equals longevity—and the veterans you're about to be tested on achieved longevity using that simple formula.

Let's find out how much you know about these veterans.

QUESTION 41: Only one player in franchise history has played 20 seasons with the Indians—this out of more than 1,700 players who have worn an Indians jersey. This veteran was also a four-time All-Star who remarkably never gave up an earned run during 13 career innings in the Mid-Summer Classic. Who is this veteran?
   a)   Mel Harder
   b)   Willis Hudlin
   c)   Steve Gromek
   d)   Mike Garcia

QUESTION 42: The Tribe won two Division Titles in three seasons with this veteran leading the offense. In that span he scored an astounding 362 runs and added 309 RBIs. He also won three Gold

Glove Awards, two Silver Slugger Awards, and made the All-Star team three consecutive seasons. Who is this veteran?
   a)   Frank Robinson
   b)   Dave Roberts
   c)   Roberto Alomar
   d)   Eddie Murray

**QUESTION 43:** This veteran third baseman played eight seasons with the Indians and had a five-year stretch in which he averaged 20 homers and made two All-Star teams—including one season when he hit 17 home runs despite being sidelined for more than a month as he battled spinal meningitis. Who is this veteran?
   a)   Casey Blake
   b)   Travis Fryman
   c)   Brook Jacoby
   d)   Max Alvis

**QUESTION 44:** This veteran second baseman had a career year in 1954 as the Indians routed the rest of the league to win the Pennant. He batted .341, which led the league and set a career high. He also established career highs with 189 hits, 112 runs, 15 home runs, and 67 RBIs that season. Who is this veteran that placed third in MVP balloting in 1954?
   a)   Johnny Berardino
   b)   Bobby Avila
   c)   Jack Conway
   d)   Bobby Young

**QUESTION 45:** This veteran was nicknamed Mr. Clutch because he batted .527 (29 for 55) with the bases loaded for the Indians. He batted a career high .326 in 1986 and he was an All-Star in 1987 when he batted .307 with 11 home runs and 86 RBIs. Who is this veteran?
   a)   Paul Sorrento
   b)   Alvaro Espinoza
   c)   Pat Tabler
   d)   Mark Lewis

**QUESTION 46:** This veteran Negro Leagues player hit 28, 27, and 31 home runs in three full seasons after joining the Tribe. He also hit a home run that traveled 477 feet into the upper deck at Cleveland Stadium—the longest recorded home run in Cleveland Stadium history. Who is this veteran?

a) Luke Easter
b) Larry Doby
c) Joe Caffie
d) Billy Harrell

**QUESTION 47:** This veteran Negro Leagues player was an All-Star and led the Newark Eagles to victory in the 1946 Negro League World Series in a hard-fought seven-game showdown vs. the Kansas City Monarchs. A year later he starred for the Indians, and the year after that he was a World Series champion. Who is this veteran?

a) Luke Easter
b) Larry Doby
c) Joe Caffie
d) Billy Harrell

**QUESTION 48:** This veteran pitcher had numerous career highlights—including the only 30-win season in franchise history and a World Series title. As if that's not impressive enough, he was also the first pitcher during the modern era of Major League history to belt a home run during the World Series. Who is this veteran?

a) Bob Lemon
b) Jim Bagby Sr.
c) Bob Feller
d) Wes Ferrell

**QUESTION 49:** These veterans share the same surname: Buddy, Gary, Jay, and Albert. Well, OK, they sort of share the same surname. Albert carried an additional letter—but whether it's "Bell" or "Belle" there's only one player in history who was dubbed "Ding Dong" because of his last name. And don't feel bad for him—Ding Dong was voted to be among the 100 greatest Indians in franchise history. Who is this veteran?

a) Buddy Bell
b) Gary Bell
c) Jay Bell
d) Albert Belle

**QUESTION 50:** A follow-up question ... Buddy, Gary, Jay and Albert all made multiple All-Star teams during their respective careers, although Jay Bell's two appearances in the Mid-Summer Classic came after he'd been traded to the National League—but only one of these veteran All-Stars was acquired by the Indians in a trade that sent away a future Hall of Famer. Who did the Indians get in the trade that sent Hall of Fame pitcher Bert Blyleven to the Minnesota Twins?

    a)   Buddy Bell
    b)   Gary Bell
    c)   Jay Bell
    d)   Albert Belle

**QUESTION 51:** The best word to describe Albert Belle during the mid-1990s is "prolific." The man could flat hit. Check out his career best season numbers in these important categories: .357 batting average (1994), 50 home runs (1995), 152 RBIs (1998, with the White Sox—his best total in Cleveland was *only* 148 RBIs in 1996), and 124 runs scored (1996). His career highs in each of these categories would contend for the league's best in any given season—and would lead the league more times than not. That being said, even with such impressive numbers there was one major title that eluded Belle throughout his career. Which title is it?

    a)   Home run
    b)   RBI
    c)   Runs
    d)   Batting

**QUESTION 52:** This veteran won league MVP honors for the only time in his career during his tenth season with the Indians, however ... despite setting career highs for runs, hits, home runs, RBIs and batting average, he did not lead the league in any of those categories during his MVP season. Who is this veteran?

    a)   Al Rosen
    b)   Lou Boudreau
    c)   George Burns
    d)   Albert Belle

**QUESTION 53:** A follow-up ... this veteran and league MVP established a franchise record when he legged out 64 doubles during his MVP campaign. Who is this veteran?
- a) Al Rosen
- b) Lou Boudreau
- c) George Burns
- d) Albert Belle

**QUESTION 54:** This veteran just got better and better with age. He averaged 31 home runs and 106 RBIs during his last four years with the Indians. In 1986 he narrowly missed joining the 30/30 club when he finished the season with 29 home runs and 29 steals. How'd he react to that? In 1987 he hit 32 home runs and stole 31 bases. Who is this veteran?
- a) Pat Tabler
- b) Mel Hall
- c) Cory Snyder
- d) Joe Carter

**QUESTION 55:** This veteran was an outstanding infielder and a popular player when he tragically died after being hit in the head by a pitch from the Yankees Carl Mays. He remains the only Major League player to die after being hit by a pitch. Who is this veteran?
- a) Doc Johnston
- b) Bill Wambsganss
- c) Ray Chapman
- d) Harry Lunte

**QUESTION 56:** Baseball is known for superstitious players and cursed teams—and at the root of every curse there's a story. Boston's curse was to trade Babe Ruth to the Yankees. Cubs fans claim a billy goat is responsible for their futility. And Cleveland's curse? The club struggled after its Pennant-winning 1954 season, but it was rich with optimism just two years later as an onslaught of new talent promised to lift the club once more to the ranks of baseball's elite—and by 1959 the club was contending for the Pennant again. And then GM Frank Lane traded this player to the Detroit Tigers and cursed everything. A team that nearly won the Pennant in 1959 couldn't even play .500 ball in 1960—and it wasn't until 1995 that the Indians managed a return trip to the postseason. And winning the World Series? Forget about it. What popular veteran did Frank Lane trade to the Tigers after the 1959 season?

a)   Minnie Minoso
b)   Jim Piersall
c)   Rocky Colavito
d)   Herb Score

**QUESTION 57:** This veteran pitcher won 24 games for the Indians in 1919. How do you top that? Well, you win another 24 games in 1920—and then pile on three more victories in the 1920 World Series. That's exactly what this pitcher did. Also, his three World Series wins? All three were complete games and he gave up just two earned runs. Total. In 27 innings against the best team in the National League. Now *that's* impressive. Who is this veteran?

a)   Ray Caldwell
b)   Stan Coveleski
c)   Guy Morton
d)   Dick Niehaus

**QUESTION 58:** This veteran batted .295 during 898 games in the first of two tours of duty with the club. After playing in Japan in 1995, he signed with the Indians for his second tour and batted .322 in 1996. Later he extended his career even more by playing in Korea and in Mexico. Who is this veteran All-Star?

a)   Julio Franco
b)   Omar Vizquel
c)   Andre Thornton
d)   Sandy Alomar Jr.

**QUESTION 59:** This pitcher signed with the Indians as a free agent in 1995. He paid immediate dividends, winning 16 games during the regular season and then posting a 4-1 record with a 1.53 earned run average during the postseason. In three seasons he totaled 45 wins and the Indians made three consecutive trips to the postseason. Who is this veteran hurler?

a)   Dennis Martinez
b)   Charles Nagy

c)   Orel Hershiser
d)   Ken Hill

**QUESTION 60:** This veteran batted just 235 times for Cleveland, hitting 14 balls out of the park. One of them was pretty special though. It came on Opening Day in his first at bat as player-manager for the Indians. It was his eighth and final Opening Day home run—a Major League record. Who is this veteran player-manager?

a)   Joe Adcock
b)   Joe Gordon
c)   Tris Speaker
d)   Frank Robinson

# 3 ANSWER KEY

| | |
|---|---|
| ___ **QUESTION 41:** A | ___ **QUESTION 51:** D* |
| ___ **QUESTION 42:** C | ___ **QUESTION 52:** B* |
| ___ **QUESTION 43:** D | ___ **QUESTION 53:** C |
| ___ **QUESTION 44:** B | ___ **QUESTION 54:** D |
| ___ **QUESTION 45:** C | ___ **QUESTION 55:** C* |
| ___ **QUESTION 46:** A | ___ **QUESTION 56:** C* |
| ___ **QUESTION 47:** B* | ___ **QUESTION 57:** B |
| ___ **QUESTION 48:** B* | ___ **QUESTION 58:** A |
| ___ **QUESTION 49:** B* | ___ **QUESTION 59:** C |
| ___ **QUESTION 50:** C* | ___ **QUESTION 60:** D* |

**KEEP A RUNNING TALLY OF YOUR CORRECT ANSWERS!**

Number correct:   ___ / 20

Overall correct:   ___ / 60

#47 – Only four players in history played in both the Negro League World Series and the Major League World Series: Doby, Monte Irvin, Willie Mays, and Satchel Paige. All four players won the Major League World Series, but only Doby, Irvin, and Paige won both titles. Mays was a 17-year-old kid when he was on the losing side of the 1948 Negro League World Series and by the time he was 20 he was in the majors with the Giants.

#48 – In addition to hitting a home run, Bagby pitched a complete game. He scattered 13 hits but gave up just one run as Cleveland beat Brooklyn 8-1 during Game 5 of the best-of-eight 1920 World Series. Cleveland won the series 5 games to 2.

#49 – Gary "Ding Dong" Bell won 96 games pitching for the Indians—a total that ranks among the top 20 in franchise history.

#50 – Keep in mind that Blyleven began his career with the Twins as well. It's not like the Indians let him get away early in his career with a bad trade. Blyleven was a veteran in his mid-30s when Cleveland traded him back to Minnesota for Jay Bell, who was a young and highly regarded prospect. But if you were Jay Bell, it'd have to be a little bit cool knowing you were traded for a Hall of Famer … right?

#51 – Belle batted .357 in 1994, second best in the league behind the .359 average that Paul O'Neill posted for the New York Yankees. Also, Belle only won one home run title in his career—this despite a five-year stretch in which he hit 50, 48, 30, 49, and 37 home runs.

#52 – Boudreau was MVP in 1948, the same season he led the Indians to victory in the World Series as player-manager—and he remains the last player-manager in MLB history to win the World Series.

#55 – Chapman died on August 17, 1920. In his ninth season with the club, he'd never played in the postseason. Almost two months to the day after his death, the Indians defeated the Brooklyn Robins to win the 1920 World Series.

#56 – Colavito was the AL home run champion in 1959 and he was traded for Harvey Kuenn, who was the AL batting champion in 1959. It was the first time in history that defending home run and batting champions were traded for each other.

#60 – Robinson became the first African-American manager in Major League history when he took over as player-manager for the Indians in 1975. In 1981 he became the first African-American manager in National League history as well, when he took over the San Francisco Giants.

*"He made his living by throwing the ball to a spot over the plate the size of a matchbook."*
— Cool Papa Bell, on his teammate and Hall of Fame legend Satchel Paige

# 4 THE LEGENDS

**HALL OF FAME** legend Bob Feller said in his induction speech, "I was just thinking a moment ago that occasionally when you're in some outlying community outside here [Cooperstown], there's been a little controversy whether the first baseball game was ever played in Cooperstown, or elsewhere. I'm not concerned where the first one was played as long as it was played, and it certainly made a great deal of difference in the lives of most all Americans." Feller, of course, is one of the many legends who made baseball our National Pastime, who used his talent and passion for a game to make a difference in the lives of generations of Americans. His induction speech was gracious, and when he spoke of himself he did so with a great deal of humility, but the words he used to describe the game capture perfectly the sentiment that generations of fans feel for the many legends who wore an Indians uniform.

There are currently 12 players enshrined as an Indian at Cooperstown: Earl Averill, Lou Boudreau, Stan Coveleski, Larry Doby, Bob Feller, Elmer Flick, Addie Joss, Nap Lajoie, Bob Lemon, Joe Sewell, Tris Speaker, and Early Wynn—and another 16 members of the Hall of Fame wore an Indians uniform at one time or another.

This chapter is all about the legends. The guys who played a game so well that it made a difference in our lives.

**QUESTION 61:** The first All-Star Game in Major League history was played on July 6, 1933, at the old Comiskey Park in Chicago. The American League, led by stars such as Babe Ruth and Lefty Gomez, won the inaugural contest, 4-2. Earl Averill, along with Ruth, was among the five outfielders that were on that team. Cleveland's star outfielder was 1 for 1 with an RBI—and then he proceeded to do something that none of the other outfielders on that All-Star squad were able to replicate: he kept making the squad again and again, year after year, setting the record for outfielders by appearing in … how many consecutive games beginning with the first ever played?

  a)   4
  b)   5
  c)   6
  d)   7

**QUESTION 62:** This Hall of Famer was pretty good on the hardwood as well as the diamond. He was a star basketball player at the University of Illinois, winning a Big Ten title and earning All-American honors before choosing a career in baseball. Who is this legend?

  a)   Lou Boudreau
  b)   Bert Blyleven
  c)   Bob Lemon
  d)   Early Wynn

**QUESTION 63:** This Hall of Famer starred alongside Ronald Reagan on the silver screen. He played the role of pitcher Jesse Haines in a movie titled *The Winning Team*. Who is this legend?

  a)   Bob Feller
  b)   Bob Lemon
  c)   Early Wynn
  d)   Hoyt Wilhelm

**QUESTION 64:** Satchel Paige made his Major League debut with the Indians on August 20, 1948, vs. the Chicago White Sox. He pitched his way to a 1-0 victory in front of 78,382 fans. The attendance mark set a record for a night baseball game that still stands today. Paige was famous for many things—of course he spent many years starring in the Negro Leagues, establishing countless records, striking out prolific numbers of hitters, throwing no-hitters, winning league titles, and entertaining crowds by the thousands with his exploits on the field and his dynamic personality and knack for storytelling off the field. And of course one of the enduring legacies of Paige's good humor and storytelling is the speculation surrounding his actual age and date of birth. According to Major League Baseball's official records, when Paige made his "rookie" debut with the Cleveland Indians he was 42-years-old. Much later, after two years with the

Indians and three years with the St. Louis Browns, Paige came out of retirement to pitch three innings in a game for the Kansas City Athletics. In that game he set a Major League record as the oldest player in history. How old was he when he appeared in one game for the Athletics?

    a)  49
    b)  53
    c)  57
    d)  59

**QUESTION 65:** Elmer Flick batted .299 during nine seasons in Cleveland, and overall the outfielder batted .313 during his Hall of Fame career. In his time with the Tribe, Flick routinely led the league in any number of categories including runs, steals, triples, and batting. In fact, Flick was so good that one team famously offered to trade another future Hall of Famer to acquire him. Who did Cleveland reject in favor of keeping Flick?

    a)  Ty Cobb
    b)  Walter Johnson
    c)  Grover Alexander
    d)  Eddie Collins

**QUESTION 66:** Cleveland was the Blues, then the Bronchos, and finally the Naps, long before they were the Indians. The Naps was in honor of Hall of Fame legend Nap Lajoie, who joined the club in 1902 and then took the reigns as player-manager in 1905, a position he held for five seasons through 1909. Lajoie batted .339 in 13 total seasons with the Indians and in his career he won five batting titles. How many batting titles did he win during the time he was player-manager for the Indians?

    a)  0
    b)  1
    c)  2
    d)  3

**QUESTION 67:** There is always an electric atmosphere on Opening Day as players and fans alike are anxious to start a new season. You get that same kind of atmosphere when a pitcher gets late into a game and he's still hanging a zero in the hit column on the scoreboard. Now imagine it's Opening Day *and* the guy on the mound is hanging a zero in the hit column ... it's happened only once in Major League history. Who pitched an Opening Day no-hitter for the Indians?

a) Dennis Eckersley
b) Len Barker
c) Bob Lemon
d) Bob Feller

**QUESTION 68:** Free agency changed the baseball landscape in many ways. It created more opportunities for players, but it also meant increasingly fewer players would spend an entire career playing for one franchise—and that's especially true for players capable of becoming "legends," the ones in such demand on the free agent market. So thanks to free agency, this one is probably a permanent record ... who played more games in an Indians uniform than any other player in franchise history?

a) Ken Keltner
b) Terry Turner
c) Omar Vizquel
d) Charlie Jamieson

**QUESTION 69:** A follow-up question ... among the numerous Hall of Fame legends who have played for the Indians, who played the most games wearing an Indians uniform?

a) Tris Speaker
b) Joe Sewell
c) Nap Lajoie
d) Earl Averill

**QUESTION 70:** Grady Sizemore won back-to-back Gold Glove Awards during 2007-08. Sizemore ended a dry spell for the Indians, as the last Gold Glove recipients were Roberto Alomar and Omar Vizquel in 2001. You have to go back even farther to find the last outfielder to win a Gold Glove prior to Sizemore—all the way to 1996. Who was a Gold Glove outfielder for the Indians in 1996?

a) Manny Ramirez
b) Kenny Lofton

c)   Albert Belle
d)   Brian Giles

**QUESTION 71:** And speaking of Gold Gloves … the first time they were awarded was 1957, and it was a year later when a member of the Indians won the award for the first time. Who was the first Gold Glove recipient in franchise history?
a)   Minnie Minoso
b)   Vic Power
c)   Jim Piersall
d)   Vic Davalillo

**QUESTION 72:** The Indians traded Bert Blyleven to the Minnesota Twins to acquire shortstop Jay Bell—which makes it a touch ironic that when Bell made his big league debut on September 29, 1986, it was against the Minnesota Twins and Blyleven was the starting pitcher. So how did Bell fare? Not only was he traded for a future Hall of Famer, but he also homered against him in his first Major League at bat. It was only the second time in franchise history that a player homered in his first career at bat. Do you know the legend who was the first in franchise history to start his career with a home run?
a)   Jim Thome
b)   Manny Ramirez
c)   George Burns
d)   Earl Averill

**QUESTION 73:** If you hit enough home runs and pick up enough RBIs that you inspire both a book and a rock-n-roll song, then you qualify as a legend, right? Who can claim this feat as a member of the Indians?
a)   Albert Belle
b)   Joe Charboneau
c)   Rocky Colavito
d)   Travis Hafner

**QUESTION 74:** Or try this: if you tie a home run record set by Babe Ruth in 1927, then do you qualify as a legend? Surely, one would think. The Great Bambino hit a Major League record 17 home runs during September 1927—the most on record for the month of September in all of baseball history. And since 1927 only one guy has hit as many as 17 home runs in the regular season's final month—and he did it for the Tribe. Who was it?

a) Albert Belle
b) Joe Charboneau
c) Rocky Colavito
d) Travis Hafner

**QUESTION 75:** Only seven guys in franchise history have collected six hits in a single nine-inning game—the first was Zaza Harvey, who did it on April 25, 1902. This modern day legend was the most recent, turning in a 6 for 7 day at the plate with a pair of doubles, three runs and four RBIs against the Yankees. Who was it?

a) Grady Sizemore
b) Omar Vizquel
c) Roberto Alomar
d) Travis Hafner

**QUESTION 76:** Sandy Alomar Jr. made big news in 1997 when he put together a 30-game hitting streak. It remains the second longest streak in franchise history and he came just one game short of tying the record set by this icon. Who hit in a franchise record 31 consecutive games?

a) Tris Speaker
b) Joe Sewell
c) Nap Lajoie
d) Lou Boudreau

**QUESTION 77:** These members of the Tribe all did something involving a home run that Hank Aaron never accomplished: Bill Bradley, Earl Averill, Odell Hale, Larry Doby, Tony Horton, and Andre Thornton. What could it possibly be? The answer: every one of them hit for the cycle. It might be hard to believe that Hank Aaron hit 755 career home runs, 624 doubles, 98 triples, and 2,294 singles, yet never managed to hit one of each in the same game—but it's true. Bradley (and his 34 career home runs) hit the first in franchise history, and Thornton hit the last of the 20th century for the Indians. There was a 25-year gap between Andre Thornton and the Indians first cycle of the 21st century. It came on August 14, 2003, one day after this player was 0 for 5 with four strikeouts. Who hit for the seventh cycle in franchise history?

a)   Milton Bradley
b)   Brandon Phillips
c)   Travis Hafner
d)   Victor Martinez

QUESTION 78: This legendary player was just the fifth in American League history with 11 consecutive 20-home run seasons—and he's also the only player in franchise history to launch four home runs in a single game. And he did it in four consecutive at bats. Who is this legend?

a)   Larry Doby
b)   Rocky Colavito
c)   Jim Thome
d)   Manny Ramirez

QUESTION 79: This player is legendary because he hit what is perhaps the most significant home run in franchise history—on the road at Fenway Park, a one-game playoff for the Pennant. No pressure, right? Tied 1-1, he hit a three-run bomb over the Green Monster for a lead that the Tribe never relinquished, winning the Pennant 8-3 and setting the stage for victory in the World Series. Who is this legend?

a)   Dale Mitchell
b)   Joe Gordon
c)   Ken Keltner
d)   Jim Hegan

QUESTION 80: The Major League record for home runs in consecutive games is eight—and only 17 players in history have homered in as many as six consecutive games. The franchise record for Cleveland is seven. Who is the legendary slugger that homered in seven consecutive games for the Tribe?

a)   Jim Thome
b)   Manny Ramirez
c)   Albert Belle
d)   Travis Hafner

# 4 ANSWER KEY

| | |
|---|---|
| ____ **QUESTION 61:** C | ____ **QUESTION 71:** B* |
| ____ **QUESTION 62:** A | ____ **QUESTION 72:** D |
| ____ **QUESTION 63:** B | ____ **QUESTION 73:** B* |
| ____ **QUESTION 64:** D | ____ **QUESTION 74:** A |
| ____ **QUESTION 65:** A* | ____ **QUESTION 75:** B* |
| ____ **QUESTION 66:** A* | ____ **QUESTION 76:** C |
| ____ **QUESTION 67:** D | ____ **QUESTION 77:** C |
| ____ **QUESTION 68:** A | ____ **QUESTION 78:** B |
| ____ **QUESTION 69:** C | ____ **QUESTION 79:** C |
| ____ **QUESTION 70:** B | ____ **QUESTION 80:** A |

KEEP A RUNNING TALLY OF YOUR CORRECT ANSWERS!

Number correct:    ____ / 20

Overall correct:    ____ / 80

#65 – In retrospect, perhaps Cleveland should have made this deal. It was offered in the spring of 1908, and after it was refused Flick became ill, missed most of the season, and never returned to his previous form or played regularly again.

#66 – Lajoie won back-to-back batting titles in 1903-04 during his first two seasons with Cleveland, but after five years as player-manager from 1905-09 he declared the extra duties required to manage the club were hurting his performance on the field. So how did he fare in 1910? After relinquishing his managerial duties he raised his average sixty points and led the league with a .384 batting average for his third title in Cleveland.

#71 – Minnie Minoso actually won a Gold Glove in 1957, the first year they were awarded—but he won it with the White Sox. He won a Gold Glove for Cleveland too, but not until 1959. Power won the award in 1958 playing first base for the Indians, and he'd go on to win it seven consecutive years from 1958-64 (the last three with the Twins). Power remains the only first baseman in franchise history to win a Gold Glove.

#73 – "Go Joe Charboneau" was inspired not only by home runs and RBIs, but also by his ability to open a beer bottle with his eye socket and then drink it through a straw in his nose. The song was a hit in Cleveland.

#75 – Vizquel's big day was August 31, 2004, and it paced a 22-0 drumming of the Yankees—on the road, in the Bronx. It was the worst beating in franchise history for the Yankees. It also set a Major League record for the largest shutout win during baseball's modern era. The game before, the Indians beat the White Sox 9-0. It was an impressive couple of games for the Indians. As for the other side, Yankees catcher Jorge Posada said it was "obviously embarrassing" and Alex Rodriguez said the Yankees should "worry about Cleveland, not about Boston." Yankees starting pitcher Javier Vazquez actually said afterwards, "I thought I had good stuff today ..." Seriously, he said it.

*"I was blessed with good eyes. I could see the ball jump off the bat."*
— Joe Sewell, Hall of Fame legend

# 5 THE HITTERS

**THE CLEVELAND INDIANS** are well represented when it comes to baseball's all-time greatest hitters. Three of the top 20 lifetime averages in baseball history belong to players who spent a significant portion of their careers in Cleveland: Joe Jackson, Tris Speaker, and Nap Lajoie. A look at the top 50 lifetime leaders in home run, hits, RBIs, and steals produces the same result—you'll find Indians up and down the leader boards. We spend a lot of time talking about the game's greats—and you'll find many of them in this chapter—but sometimes the best conversations are about hitters who are defined by a spectacular season or a single great moment, rather than an entire career.

For example: Larry Gardner won four world championships (three with Boston, one with Cleveland) and batted .289 during parts of 17 big league seasons, but as a hitter his career isn't defined by leader boards. Playing primarily in the dead ball era, Gardner hit just 27 career home runs in 1,923 games—but somehow he managed to hit three home runs in 25 games during World Series play. At that rate he should have hit 230-plus home runs in his career. You see how Gardner can make for an interesting conversation?

Or how about this: Gardner hit just three home runs in 1920, yet managed *118 RBIs*. Then he hit three home runs again in 1921, only this time he set a career high with *120 RBIs*. Gardner also took it upon himself to steal three bases during his spectacular season in 1920. And now you're thinking, three steals isn't very spectacular … and you're right, because what is *really spectacular* is that he was thrown out trying to steal 20 times that same season, yet somehow he had it in his head that he should keep on running.

More fun conversations:

Joe DiMaggio batted safely in 56 consecutive games in 1941, the same season Ted Williams batted .406—but did you know that also in 1941, Jeff Heath, an outfielder who spent a decade playing for the

Indians, became the first player in AL history to hit 20 doubles, 20 triples, and 20 home runs in the same season? It's true.

What about Dick Howser? A World Series champion as manager of the Kansas City Royals in 1985, two decades earlier he was the Indians shortstop—and I'm assuming he was a really good fielding shortstop, because during 107 games and 377 plate appearances, Howser managed *only six RBIs*. And yes, he did hit a home run (he was the antithesis of Larry Gardner, I guess)—and yes, futility can also be spectacular, as long as it's futile enough. You see?

And one more: Joe Sewell is the toughest strikeout in baseball history. In 14 seasons he struck out only 114 times—he never struck out three times in a game, and he struck out twice in a game on only two occasions. So how is it possible that a 30-year-old pitcher who won eight games and recorded 54 strikeouts—*in his career*—fanned Sewell twice in one game? I don't know, but he did, in 1923.

And now for the trivia—all-time greats, spectacular seasons, and great moments, this chapter is all about the hitters.

**QUESTION 81:** Our first question is about an all-time great who shows up on numerous leader boards. Who was the first player to record his 3,000th career hit while wearing a Cleveland uniform?
- a) Tris Speaker
- b) Nap Lajoie
- c) Eddie Murray
- d) Roberto Alomar

**QUESTION 82:** Acquired by the Indians in a trade that sent Joe Carter to the San Diego Padres, this guy is the definition of a professional hitter. In a four-year span from 1992-95, he hit .316 with 75 home runs, 389 RBIs, 365 runs, and 44 steals—and for good measure he batted .292 with nine RBIs during the 1995 postseason. Who is this hitter?
- a) Brian Giles
- b) Paul Sorrento
- c) Carlos Baerga
- d) Candy Maldonado

**QUESTION 83:** This slugger hit a crucial home run in the 1948 World Series. The Boston Braves had seized the early advantage by winning Game 1, but the Indians rallied to take Games 2 and 3. Then in Game 4, in a fiercely contested pitcher's duel, his third-inning blast proved to be the difference in a 2-1 Indians victory that paved the way for the club to win the series in six games. Who came up clutch in Game 4 of the 1948 World Series?

    a)   Larry Doby
    b)   Eddie Robinson
    c)   Joe Gordon
    d)   Dale Mitchell

**QUESTION 84:** The legendary Shoeless Joe Jackson batted .375 during parts of six seasons with the Indians. In his 1911 rookie campaign he batted .408, and in his sophomore campaign he batted .395—that gave him a combined .402 average after two big league seasons, by far the highest in Major League history. Jackson hit a more pedestrian .373 in 1913, and fans must have been maniacs, booing and heckling like crazy when he batted *only* .338 in 1914. Jackson was traded to the White Sox after 83 games in 1915. He was batting a paltry .327 at the time. So ... how many career batting titles did Jackson win?

    a)   0
    b)   1
    c)   2
    d)   3

**QUESTION 85:** Shortstops have historically been light hitting—defense first, and anything at the plate was a bonus. Ernie Banks was not the norm, far from it. It wasn't until Cal Ripken Jr. came along that big guys who could hit the ball a mile began to gain acceptance around baseball. So in terms of offense, this Indians shortstop was a trailblazer of sorts—he was the first shortstop in American League history to bat over .350 with more than 100 RBIs in a single season. Who was he?

    a)   Dick Howser
    b)   Ray Boone
    c)   Roger Peckinpaugh
    d)   Lou Boudreau

**QUESTION 86:** Only 14 players in baseball's modern era have won the batting Triple Crown—leading the league in average, home runs, and RBIs in the same season. Cleveland has never had a Triple Crown winner, but this slugger came close. In fact, no one has ever come closer without actually winning. He led the league in home runs and RBIs and when he stepped to the plate for his 688th and final plate appearance of the season, if he'd gotten a base hit then he would have led the league in batting and claimed the Triple Crown ... instead he grounded out. Who is this slugger?

    a)   Manny Ramirez
    b)   Albert Belle
    c)   Al Rosen
    d)   Earl Averill

**QUESTION 87:** This one falls into the "spectacular but dubious" category. This player is the only one in Major League history to post three consecutive seasons with 25 or more home runs, and yet ... he failed to reach 100 home runs for his career. Three consecutive seasons with 25-plus home runs, spectacular—93 career home runs, all things considered, a bit disappointing. Who had consecutive seasons of 28, 27, and 31 home runs for the Indians but retired with only 93 bombs after parts of six Major League seasons?

    a)   Leon Wagner
    b)   Luke Easter
    c)   Fred Whitfield
    d)   Jim Hegan

**QUESTION 88:** Spectacular doesn't come close to describing how this player performed during August 2006. For the month he batted .361, including a 14-game hitting streak, and he led the world with 13 home runs and 30 RBIs. The club had been struggling to play .500 until this guy strapped the team onto his shoulders and carried them to 14 wins in 18 games, and a season best 18-10 record for the month. He was obviously the AL Player of the Month, but even that pales in comparison with something else he did during this ridiculous hot streak: he blasted his sixth grand slam of the season, tying Yankees legend Don Mattingly for the Major League record. Who was nothing short of prodigious at the plate in August 2006?

a)  Victor Martinez
b)  Grady Sizemore
c)  Casey Blake
d)  Travis Hafner

**QUESTION 89:** Let's check out those leader boards we mentioned in the intro, starting with the franchise record books. Who ranks first in franchise history for highest single-season home run total and career home runs?

a)  Jim Thome
b)  Albert Belle
c)  Manny Ramirez
d)  Travis Hafner

**QUESTION 90:** Hal Trosky had some unbelievable numbers in the mid-1930s. The powerful first baseman had 142 RBIs as a 21-year-old rookie in 1934. He backed it up with 113, 162, 128, 110, and 104 RBIs from 1935-39. He ranged from 19 to a high of 42 homers in that stretch and he was one of the most feared hitters in the game. His 162 RBIs in 1936 stood as the franchise single-season record until Manny Ramirez eclipsed it with 165 RBIs in 1999. But does either of these players hold the franchise record for career RBIs? Here are your choices:

a)  Hal Trosky
b)  Manny Ramirez
c)  Jim Thome
d)  Earl Averill

**QUESTION 91:** A few questions back we asked about the first man in franchise history to notch career hit 3,000 in an Indians uniform— but how about this? No player has accumulated all 3,000 hits required to join that elite fraternity while wearing an Indians uniform, in fact, the franchise record for hits is 2,046. Who is the legendary hitter that holds this franchise record?

a)  Tris Speaker
b)  Nap Lajoie
c)  Earl Averill
d)  Joe Sewell

**QUESTION 92:** Grady Sizemore made a run at a franchise record in 2006 when he banged out 92 extra-base hits. He came up a few short of the record 103 established by this powerful hitter. Who holds the Indians single-season record for extra-base hits?

  a)  Hal Trosky
  b)  Manny Ramirez
  c)  Jim Thome
  d)  Albert Belle

**QUESTION 93:** This legendary hitter holds the franchise season record with 140 runs scored, and he also holds the franchise career record with 1,154 runs. Including the top spot, he holds three of the ten highest scoring seasons on record in franchise history. Who is this outstanding hitter?

  a)  Kenny Lofton
  b)  Tris Speaker
  c)  Earl Averill
  d)  Omar Vizquel

**QUESTION 94:** Tris Speaker posted five of the ten highest season batting averages in franchise history—and despite batting .378 or higher in each of those five seasons, his career average with the Indians is only the second highest in franchise history. Who holds the franchise record for career batting average?

  a)  Joe Jackson
  b)  Nap Lajoie
  c)  Lew Fonseca
  d)  George Burns

**QUESTION 95:** Sandy Alomar Jr. had a hot week back in 1997 in which he posted back-to-back four-hit games. Quite an impressive feat for anyone, but especially for a catcher—considering the wear and tear on his body and the unlikely event that he'd beat out a close play at first for an infield hit. A catcher who bangs out four base knocks in a game usually gets them legit. It wasn't until a full decade later that another Indians catcher posted back-to-back four-hit games—and it couldn't have come at a better time. He was batting .236 in mid-July, but started coming around and raised his average to .268 on August 1. And then he really caught fire—a 13-game hitting streak with eight multi-hit games, followed a week later by back-to-back four-hit games had his average all the way up to .295 and still climbing. That same week he was 15 for 28 with three home runs, six RBIs, eight runs scored, and he was named AL Player of the Week in a no-brainer vote. Who is the catcher that caught fire and replicated Alomar's impressive feat a full decade later?

   a)  Einar Diaz
   b)  Josh Bard
   c)  Kelly Shoppach
   d)  Victor Martinez

**QUESTION 96:** This player once hit a ball rather famously that was later described as such: "It would have been a home run in any other park—including Yellowstone." Instead, he's remembered as the guy who got robbed by Willie Mays spectacular catch during the 1954 World Series between the Indians and the Giants, a play that remains one of the game's all-time greatest defensive efforts. What people often forget about this player is that his greatest battle wasn't that one at bat, and that one out never defined his career. He was stricken with polio in 1955, and after 74 games his season was over and his career was hanging in the balance. "The Catch" by Willie Mays couldn't keep him down, and neither could polio—he came back in 1956, and despite playing in only 136 games he belted 32 home runs with 106 RBIs. And then he backed them up with 28 home runs and 105 RBIs in 1957. Who is this great hitter that refused to let adversity keep him on the sidelines?

   a)  Bobby Avila
   b)  George Strickland
   c)  Al Smith
   d)  Vic Wertz

**QUESTION 97:** You read earlier about the slugger who homered in seven consecutive games for the Indians. Well, one of his teammates nearly tied that record after homering in six consecutive games. Who fell two short of tying the MLB record and just one short of tying the franchise record for consecutive games with a home run?

   a)  Jim Thome
   b)  Manny Ramirez

c)   Albert Belle
d)   Travis Hafner

**QUESTION 98:** Manny Acta called this player "a one-man wrecking crew" after he hit a three-run eighth-inning homer to beat the Rangers 3-2, then two days later he hit an eighth-inning double to drive in the go-ahead run in a victory vs. the White Sox, and the very next day he hit a grand slam with five RBIs to pace Cleveland's 7-4 victory against the White Sox. All total he was 11 for 19 in six games that week, along with three home runs and 11 RBIs. And it was only the second week of the season. Who got off to such a hot start in 2010, earned AL Player of the Week honors, and carried the club to four straight wins that erased an early deficit in the Division standings?
a)   Asdrubal Cabrera
b)   Jhonny Peralta
c)   Shin-Soo Choo
d)   Austin Kearns

**QUESTION 99:** The Indians and Tigers were battling for the top spot in the Division standings during the early part of 2007, so when they met for a three-game series in May it was considered a pivotal series that could shape the direction of the rest of the season. All this player did was lead the Indians to a clean sweep of the Tigers, hitting two home runs, drawing four walks, and scoring four runs in the series. For the week he had eight hits in six games, but every one of his hits went for extra-bases—four home runs, three doubles, and a triple. He also scored eight runs, had eight RBIs, and six walks. Manager Eric Wedge understated things a touch, saying of this player, "I'm very happy." Although he couldn't contain the grin on his face as he said it. For his efforts this player was named AL Player of the Week and the Indians gained sole possession of first place in the AL Central and pretty much stayed there the rest of the season. Who is he?
a)   Casey Blake
b)   Trot Nixon
c)   Grady Sizemore
d)   Jason Michaels

**QUESTION 100:** Talk about a beat down … Cleveland beat Oakland 20-6 on May 4, 1991, and then backed it up with a 15-6 thrashing against Oakland the very next day. This player had a career day during the game on May 4, contributing to the Indians 20-run outburst by going 4 for 5 at the plate with two home runs, three runs scored, and a franchise record *nine RBIs*. Both home runs were of the three-run variety, and he added a two-run single and an RBI single to account for his nine total RBIs. Oh, in his first 19 games of the season … five total RBIs. But after his big day, he'd driven in 14 runs in only 20 games. Sounds much better, don't you think? Who is this hitter?

    a)   Mark Whiten
    b)   Chris James
    c)   Albert Belle
    d)   Brook Jacoby

# 5 ANSWER KEY

___ **QUESTION 81:** B          ___ **QUESTION 91:** B
___ **QUESTION 82:** C          ___ **QUESTION 92:** D
___ **QUESTION 83:** A          ___ **QUESTION 93:** C
___ **QUESTION 84:** A          ___ **QUESTION 94:** A
___ **QUESTION 85:** D          ___ **QUESTION 95:** D
___ **QUESTION 86:** C*         ___ **QUESTION 96:** D
___ **QUESTION 87:** B*         ___ **QUESTION 97:** D
___ **QUESTION 88:** D          ___ **QUESTION 98:** C
___ **QUESTION 89:** A          ___ **QUESTION 99:** A
___ **QUESTION 90:** D          ___ **QUESTION 100:** B

**KEEP A RUNNING TALLY OF YOUR CORRECT ANSWERS!**

Number correct:    ___ / 20

Overall correct:    ___ / 100

#86 – Mickey Vernon won the batting title for the Washington Senators after beating out a bunt single on the season's final day. The story goes that the Philadelphia Athletics third baseman made little to no effort at actually trying to throw out Vernon—and true or not, the story continues that some of Vernon's teammates made outs intentionally to prevent him from having to bat again and potentially make an out. Rosen's last at bat resulted in a bang-bang play at first, but the call went against him and he lost the Triple Crown by .001611787 percentage points.

#87 – OK, this one's a little misleading. Easter was a star in the Negro Leagues who hit countless home runs before debuting as a 33-year-old "rookie" with the Indians.

*"I just reared back and let them go."*
— Bob Feller, Hall of Fame legend

# 6 THE PITCHERS

**THE CLEVELAND INDIANS** are also well represented when it comes to baseball's all-time greatest pitchers—just as with the hitters. A glance at yearly leader boards finds guys like Lee and Sabathia in recent years—and when you pore through the greatest records in MLB history you'll find Hall of Fame legends like Stan Coveleski, Bob Feller, Addie Joss, Bob Lemon and Early Wynn. And we treat our pitchers just as we do our hitters—we spend time talking about the greats, but we love talking about those who are defined by spectacular seasons or moments (good or bad) just as much as we love talking about those who starred for an entire career.

Some examples from the mound:

Most of us would give anything for the chance to play just one day of MLB baseball—especially for our favorite team. Well, there once was a pitcher named Bock Baker who actually got two opportunities to pitch in the big leagues. He took the mound for Cleveland against the Chicago White Sox in his big league debut. How did he fare? Well, he pitched a complete game. Pretty spectacular, right? Well, sure—but it depends on your perspective. He gave up 23 hits and 13 runs (OK, in fairness, only five of them were earned, but *he did* walk six batters…) as Chicago pounded Cleveland, 13-1. Baker never pitched for Cleveland again, but the Philadelphia Athletics gave him a second big league start that same year (1901). He lasted juts six innings, and lost again after giving up 11 runs—and then his career was over.

Debuts often are not that catastrophic. In fact, sometimes they're spectacular in all the right ways. Consider Vean Gregg, who won 23, 20 and 20 games for Cleveland during his first three big league seasons. Spectacular, for sure—but then the Indians traded him to Boston and the magical run ended. Gregg won exactly 20 games the rest of his career (five seasons, four different teams).

It's obviously fun and interesting to talk about pitchers like Baker and Gregg because "spectacular" really does cut both ways.

Then you have a guy like George Uhle, who once pitched a complete game shutout as a rookie. Big deal, you say? Well, how about: *it was a 20-inning complete game shutout?* Spectacular, I'd say. Uhle had more spectacular moments in his career. He'd later pitch a 19-inning complete game as well. His success wasn't limited to the mound. He once drove in six runs in a game, and two years later he established a Major League record for pitchers when he got 52 hits in one season.

Another spectacular feat: Dutch Levsen pitched complete games in both ends of a doubleheader on August 28, 1926, the last pitcher of the 20th century to accomplish that feat.

And finally, spectacular but dubious: Tom Candiotti, Scott Bailes, and Phil Niekro all tied for the team lead in wins in 1987. Spectacular, right? Uh, dubious—as they each won just seven games, setting a record for futility as it was the lowest total to lead a staff in wins in Major League history.

And now for the trivia—all-time greats, spectacular seasons, and great moments, this chapter is all about the pitchers.

**QUESTION 101:** A complete game from a team's starting pitcher has become a rarity in today's game, but this pitcher did something in 1986 that was a complete throwback to the first half of the 20th century—he led the league with 17 complete games, a total that was one more than the career high 16 games he won that same season. Just a few decades earlier it was common for starting pitchers to total more complete games than wins, but these days it almost never happens. Who was the starting pitcher that completed more games than he won in 1986?

    a)   Tom Candiotti
    b)   Ken Schrom
    c)   Don Schulze
    d)   Neal Heaton

**QUESTION 102:** This Hall of Famer actually debuted professionally as a position player, spending time as both an outfielder and an infielder. It wasn't until after eight professional seasons that he embarked on his career as a pitcher. Who is he?

a) Addie Joss
b) Bob Feller
c) Bob Lemon
d) Early Wynn

**QUESTION 103:** This Hall of Famer once said, "If it hadn't been for baseball I probably would have spent my life picking corn in Iowa." He was a dominant pitcher, as evidenced by his Major League record 12 one-hitters—a feat that was later tied by fellow legend Nolan Ryan. Who is he?

a) Addie Joss
b) Bob Feller
c) Bob Lemon
d) Early Wynn

**QUESTION 104:** And speaking of one-hitters ... this Hall of Famer set a Major League record when he tossed three one-hitters in the same season. Who is he?

a) Addie Joss
b) Bob Feller
c) Bob Lemon
d) Early Wynn

**QUESTION 105:** This pitcher was the first in franchise history to win the Cy Young Award. He led the league with 24 victories and posted an incredible 1.92 earned run average with 234 strikeouts. Who is he?

a) Early Wynn
b) Gaylord Perry
c) CC Sabathia
d) Cliff Lee

**QUESTION 106:** League Park was home to the original NL Cleveland Spiders back in 1890, and it was the original home to the Indians franchise as well. The club moved to Cleveland Municipal Stadium in 1932, and stayed there until 1993. The first game at Cleveland Stadium was on July 31, 1932, and the starting pitcher was brilliant despite suffering a 1-0 loss to the Philadelphia Athletics and Hall of Famer Lefty Grove. Sixty-one years later, that same pitcher was on hand to throw the ceremonial first pitch on October 3, 1993, for the final game to be played at that ballpark (the Indians moved to Jacobs field to start 1994). Who was the pitcher that "opened" and "closed" the Indians time at Cleveland Municipal Stadium?

a)   Wes Ferrell
b)   Mel Harder
c)   Monte Pearson
d)   Thornton Lee

**QUESTION 107:** Pitch count wouldn't have been a problem for this hurler—it took him just 74 pitches to notch a complete game victory vs. the Chicago White Sox. It helped, of course, that no one reached base against him. That's right—a perfect game, the first in franchise history, and he did it against a future Hall of Fame opponent on the mound for Chicago. Who was the first pitcher in franchise history to throw a perfect game?

a)   Len Barker
b)   Bob Feller
c)   Bob Lemon
d)   Addie Joss

**QUESTION 108:** This pitcher set a franchise record for saves in spectacular fashion—because not only did he lead the league, he also had more saves *than any other team in baseball.* As in, take any other team and combine all the saves for every pitcher on its staff, and they still didn't save as many games as this closer did for the Indians. Who is he?

a)   Doug Jones
b)   Bob Wickman
c)   Jose Mesa
d)   Joe Borowski

**QUESTION 109:** CC Sabathia was 19-7 for the Indians when he won the 2007 Cy Young Award, and the balloting wasn't all that close. Josh Beckett was the league's only 20-game winner, but he placed second in the balloting with 11 fewer first place votes than Sabathia. John Lackey was 19-9 for the Angels, but placed third in the balloting and received only one first place vote. The pitcher who placed fourth in balloting that year was 19-8, and he also pitched for the Indians. He won the same number of games as Sabathia and his earned run

average was lower, but he didn't receive any first place votes. Who was fourth in balloting during CC Sabathia's Cy Young season?
   a)   Cliff Lee
   b)   Jake Westbrook
   c)   Paul Byrd
   d)   Roberto Hernandez

**QUESTION 110:** There's bound to be nerves involved for every player as he steps on the field for his big league debut, and it's probably worse if you're a teenager. Well, it wasn't a problem for this pitcher, who debuted with a scoreless inning of relief just weeks after his high school graduation. A month later he made his first big league start and fanned 15 batters on his way to a complete game 1-0 victory. Three weeks after that he tossed his third complete game in five starts, this time striking out 17. Who was this fearless teenager?
   a)   Luis Tiant
   b)   Bob Feller
   c)   Herb Score
   d)   Sam McDowell

**QUESTION 111:** Cliff Lee was so good in his 2008 Cy Young season that he was twice AL Pitcher of the Month after posting identical 5-0 records in April and August. When he beat the Royals on September 12, Lee improved to 22-2 and became the first pitcher since Bob Welch in 1990 to have 20 more wins than he did losses. His victory against Kansas City also gave him eight wins in his last eight starts, it was his 11th consecutive victorious decision, and it made him unbeaten in 12 consecutive starts overall. Who was the last pitcher (prior to Lee in 2008) to win as many as 11 consecutive decisions in one season for the Indians?
   a)   CC Sabathia
   b)   Sam McDowell
   c)   Gaylord Perry
   d)   Luis Tiant

**QUESTION 112:** Cliff Lee's phenomenal 2008 season gave the Indians a 20-game winner for the first time in 34 years. For a franchise rich in pitching tradition, it's hard to imagine, yet true. Who was the last 20-game winner for the Indians prior to 2008?

a) Gaylord Perry
b) Dick Donovan
c) Luis Tiant
d) Sam McDowell

**QUESTION 113:** The Tribe boasts many players who were 20-game winners on several occasions—but the franchise record is seven seasons with 20 or more wins. Can you name this hurler?
a) Early Wynn
b) Bob Lemon
c) Bob Feller
d) Wes Ferrell

**QUESTION 114:** This pitcher is the franchise leader in shutouts. Incredibly, he pitched a shutout in 45 of his 160 wins for the Indians … which explains why he is also the franchise leader in earned run average. Who is the Indians career leader in both shutouts and ERA?
a) Early Wynn
b) Addie Joss
c) Stan Coveleski
d) George Uhle

**QUESTION 115:** Chris Perez has been rapidly climbing the franchise leader board for career saves since taking over as the closer in 2010. He saved 23 games that season and backed them up with 36 in 2011, and a career best 39 in 2012. That puts him in the top five in franchise history after only three seasons closing for the Tribe. Who is the franchise leader with 139 saves that Perez is chasing?
a) Doug Jones
b) Jose Mesa
c) Michael Jackson
d) Bob Wickman

**QUESTION 116:** Bob Feller set a franchise record with 348 strikeouts in 1946 and he's also the career leader for the Indians with 2,581 Ks. The man second on the career list fanned 2,159 batters for the Tribe—and he also posted the second, third, fourth, and fifth highest season totals in franchise history, and twice he topped 300 Ks in a season. Who is this pitcher?

a) Early Wynn
b) Bob Lemon
c) Sam McDowell
d) Luis Tiant

**QUESTION 117:** Bob Feller also holds the franchise record with 266 career wins—including a career best 27 in 1940, a total that is tied for the second highest season effort in franchise history. Two other pitchers have won as many as 200 games for the Indians—can you pick out the pair that rank second and third in franchise history for wins?

a) Bob Lemon, Early Wynn
b) Early Wynn, Mel Harder
c) Addie Joss, Stan Coveleski
d) Mel Harder, Bob Lemon

**QUESTION 118:** You know all about how dominant Cliff Lee was in 2008. You know he was 22-3 on the season and he easily won the Cy Young Award. But do you know if Lee's 2008 campaign was good enough to produce the best single-season winning percentage in franchise history? Who holds this record?

a) Cliff Lee
b) Bob Feller
c) Johnny Allen
d) Ray Narleski

**QUESTION 119:** You've read about no-hitters and perfect games, but what about guys who are consistently tough to hit for an entire season? The franchise record for fewest hits per nine innings in a season is an astounding 5.295. Who holds this record?

a) Herb Score
b) Cliff Lee
c) Luis Tiant
d) Sam McDowell

**QUESTION 120:** You read earlier that one pitcher is the franchise career leader for both shutouts and earned run average—but the franchise record for shutouts in one season is ten, and it's been done on two occasions. Can you pick out the pair of pitchers who each had a season with ten shutouts for the Indians?

- a) Addie Joss, Luis Tiant
- b) Bob Feller, Bob Lemon
- c) Gaylord Perry, Jim Bagby Sr.
- d) Stan Coveleski, Otto Hess

# 6 ANSWER KEY

| | |
|---|---|
| ___ **QUESTION 101:** A | ___ **QUESTION 111:** C* |
| ___ **QUESTION 102:** C | ___ **QUESTION 112:** A |
| ___ **QUESTION 103:** B | ___ **QUESTION 113:** B |
| ___ **QUESTION 104:** A* | ___ **QUESTION 114:** B |
| ___ **QUESTION 105:** B* | ___ **QUESTION 115:** D |
| ___ **QUESTION 106:** B | ___ **QUESTION 116:** C |
| ___ **QUESTION 107:** D* | ___ **QUESTION 117:** D |
| ___ **QUESTION 108:** C* | ___ **QUESTION 118:** C* |
| ___ **QUESTION 109:** D* | ___ **QUESTION 119:** C* |
| ___ **QUESTION 110:** B | ___ **QUESTION 120:** B |

**KEEP A RUNNING TALLY OF YOUR CORRECT ANSWERS!**

Number correct:     ___ / 20

Overall correct:     ___ / 120

#104 – Joss tossed three one-hitters in 1907 to establish the record. Grover Alexander pitched four one-hitters in 1915 for the Philadelphia Phillies in the NL to establish a new MLB record. Dave Stieb pitched three one-hitters in 1988 for the Toronto Blue Jays to tie Joss for what remains an AL record.

#105 – Perry was the 1972 AL Cy Young winner. He later won the 1978 NL Cy Young Award, pitching for the San Diego Padres, making him the first player in history to win the award in both leagues.

#107 – Joss was perfect just one year after his record-setting three one-hitters. And just two years later he tossed another no-hitter against the White Sox. Sadly, his career ended suddenly when he contracted tubercular meningitis in 1910, just weeks after his second no-hitter—and less than a year later he passed away.

#108 – Mesa saved a franchise record 46 games in 1995. And don't forget, the schedule was reduced to 144 games that season because of the work stoppage that halted play in 1994 and eventually cancelled the 1994 postseason and threatened the 1995 regular season.

#109 – You might remember Hernandez better as Fausto Carmona, the name he played under when he claimed to be 23-years-old in 2007. Turns out he was really 26 that season.

#111 – Perry won 15 straight decisions for the Indians in 1974.

#118 – Allen (.938, 15-1, 1937), Narleski (.900, 9-1, 1955), Lee (22-3, .880, 2008) are the top three in franchise history—Feller's best season winning percentage was .813 during his 13-3 campaign in 1954, good for sixth best in franchise history.

#119 – Tiant gave up just 152 hits in 258-plus innings of work in 1968.

*"They say anything can happen in a short series. I just didn't expect it to be that short."*
— Al Lopez, Hall of Fame manager

# 7 THE MANAGERS AND COACHES

**THE CLEVELAND INDIANS** named Manny Acta as the club's new manager in October 2009. Officially he was the 40th manager in franchise history, although 44 different coaches have guided the club for at least one game—though literally, in some cases it *was* one game and strictly on an interim basis. In three seasons, Acta managed 482 games and as 2012 drew to a close he was on the threshold of ranking among the top ten in franchise history for games managed— but he was also fast approaching another threshold, as in the overwhelming majority of the club's managers were with the club for either one season, or … three seasons.

Only 12 managers have lasted more than three years with the Indians, and only three of those who did last longer than three years managed to do so without a winning record. The Indians have made strides in many areas the last three years and the shifts and changes amongst the coaching staff resulted in a highly respected group that was anxious and ready to guide the Tribe back to the postseason, but unfortunately it never materialized. Turns out the three-year threshold is a pretty solid limit for how patient an organization is when it comes to managers, and the gains made in 2011 were completely lost and then some in 2012. Acta's tenure with the club came to an end with six games left on the 2012 schedule. He ranks 13th in franchise history for games managed, but any optimism regarding the Tribe in 2013 will rest squarely with new hire Terry Francona.

Cleveland's new manager seems to have passed his first test already—longtime player, coach, and fan-favorite Sandy Alomar Jr. interviewed for the managerial job as well, and Francona's hiring could potentially have caused a rift. Francona's first act as manager was to reach out to Alomar personally and ask him to stay on the Tribe's staff for 2013. It's a pretty safe bet that Alomar will earn an opportunity to manage at the big league level in the future, but keeping him on the Tribe's staff during this transition seems vital for any success the club hopes to achieve in 2013. As for hiring Francona, general manager Chris Antonetti had this to say: "It's the first important step. Obviously we needed to make sure we got the right leader in place for our team and organization moving forward. That was our first priority. We feel Terry will be a very successful manager."

**QUESTION 121:** The Indians have won five Pennants under the leadership of four different managers: Tris Speaker, Lou Boudreau, Al Lopez, and Mike Hargrove. Who is the only manager in franchise history to win two Pennants?
- a) Tris Speaker
- b) Lou Boudreau
- c) Al Lopez
- d) Mike Hargrove

**QUESTION 122:** This manager had an outstanding collegiate career as he led the Wichita State Shockers to victory in the College World Series and was selected in the third round of the draft by the Boston Red Sox. Later, as manager of the Indians he won a Division Title and took home AL Manager of the Year honors. Who is he?
- a) Eric Wedge
- b) Joel Skinner
- c) Manny Acta
- d) Charlie Manuel

**QUESTION 123:** This manager spent a significant portion of his playing career with the Indians, and later he won AL Manager of the Year honors after leading the club to the second highest season winning percentage in franchise history. Who is he?
- a) Eric Wedge
- b) Joel Skinner
- c) Manny Acta
- d) Mike Hargrove

**QUESTION 124:** The highest season winning percentage in franchise history is an astounding .721—one of the best in baseball history—

but unfortunately it belongs to the 1954 team that was swept in the World Series. Who managed the Indians to a franchise record 111 regular season victories and a .721 winning percentage before falling in the World Series?

  a) Lou Boudreau
  b) Al Lopez
  c) Kerby Farrell
  d) Joe Gordon

**QUESTION 125:** Only four men in franchise history have managed the Indians for more than 1,000 games: Mike Hargrove, Lou Boudreau, Eric Wedge, and Tris Speaker. Which of these managers holds the franchise records for both games managed and victories?

  a) Mike Hargrove
  b) Lou Boudreau
  c) Eric Wedge
  d) Tris Speaker

**QUESTION 126:** A follow-up … just because a manager has the most victories there's no guarantee that he's also the leader in terms of winning percentage. So, among the managers with 1,000 games at the helm for the Tribe, who has the highest career winning percentage?

  a) Mike Hargrove
  b) Lou Boudreau
  c) Eric Wedge
  d) Tris Speaker

**QUESTION 127:** In a previous chapter you read about Frank Robinson, who homered in his first at bat as player-manager for the Indians. There have been some pretty nice accomplishments by Indians player-managers—including this one, who collected his 3,000th career hit while managing the Tribe. Who is he?

  a) Nap Lajoie
  b) Tris Speaker
  c) Frank Robinson
  d) Joe Sewell

**QUESTION 128:** Like any other club, the Tribe has experienced ups and downs—a few good years knocking on postseason's door followed by long dry spells with no illusions of postseason glory. Only one manager in franchise history has accomplished this feat, however—he led the Tribe to the playoffs in five consecutive seasons. Who is he?

a)  Mike Hargrove
b)  Lou Boudreau
c)  Eric Wedge
d)  Tris Speaker

**QUESTION 129:** One of the most successful managers in franchise history, he holds the club record for most games above .500 with 216—meaning he won 216 more games than he lost, which is easily the highest number in franchise history. Additionally, his worst finish as Indians manager: second place. Who is he?

a)  Al Lopez
b)  Mike Hargrove
c)  Lou Boudreau
d)  Nap Lajoie

**QUESTION 130:** Conversely, this manager has the uncomfortable record for most games below .500 in franchise history—he lost 75 more games than he won. Additionally, his best finish as Indians manager: fifth place. Who is he?

a)  Al Dark
b)  Jeff Torborg
c)  Pat Corrales
d)  John McNamara

**QUESTION 131:** Manny Acta became the 40th manager in franchise history when he was hired in October 2009. The Indians struggled in 2010, but the former Nationals manager guided the club well in 2011 and improved the Indians record by 11 games in his second season at the helm—which was the fifth largest improvement in MLB in 2011. What place did the 2011 Indians finish in the AL Central under Manny Acta?

a)  First
b)  Second
c)  Third
d)  Fourth

**QUESTION 132:** This member of the 2012 Indians coaching staff has a son who plays minor league ball in the Tigers organization and a son who plays minor league ball in the Indians organization. As for his own career, he made it to The Show for 58 games and hit exactly one career home run. Hey, he made it, and he hit one, right? And since he hung up his playing spikes, he's done exceptionally well coaching—he was the Midwest League Manager of the Year twice and he took over his current coaching duties with the Indians in June 2011, taking on the same role he filled for three years with the Detroit Tigers from 2003-05. Who is he?
   a)   Ruben Niebla
   b)   Steve Smith
   c)   Dave Miller
   d)   Bruce Fields

**QUESTION 133:** Scott Radinsky was the Tribe's pitching coach when the 2012 season got underway, but he was replaced in August as the staff earned run average ballooned to second highest in the league. The coach who replaced him on an "interim" basis was in his 12th season with the organization and was the pitching coach for the Triple-A Columbus Clippers in 2011 and 2012. Who is this coach?
   a)   Ruben Niebla
   b)   Steve Smith
   c)   Dave Miller
   d)   Bruce Fields

**QUESTION 134:** This member of the Indians 2012 coaching staff was once upon a time Manny Acta's minor league manager. Who managed the Indians manager in Double-A ball back in 1989?
   a)   Steve Smith
   b)   Dave Miller
   c)   Tom Wiedenbauer
   d)   Bruce Fields

**QUESTION 135:** This member of the Indians 2012 coaching staff won a World Series ring while coaching for the Philadelphia Phillies. How did he celebrate? He took a trip around the world with his daughter as competitors on the hit reality show *The Amazing Race*. They only placed sixth in the race, but no worries—back in his everyday life he's renowned throughout baseball for his ability to teach fielding, as evidenced by Gold Glove recipients like Mark Teixeira, Alex Rodriguez, and Jimmy Rollins, who all give him credit for their success. Who is this coach?

    a)   Steve Smith
    b)   Dave Miller
    c)   Tom Wiedenbauer
    d)   Bruce Fields

**Question 136:** Cleveland began play as a charter member of the American League in 1901 and this manager has the distinction of being the first in franchise history. Who led the club to a 54-82 record during its first year of play in 1901?

    a)   Nap Lajoie
    b)   Deacon McGuire
    c)   Jimmy McAleer
    d)   Bill Armour

**QUESTION 137:** This manager wasn't the first in franchise history, but he was the first manager in franchise history to lead the club into the postseason. Who was the first Pennant-winning manager for the Indians?

    a)   Tris Speaker
    b)   Lee Fohl
    c)   Roger Peckinpaugh
    d)   Nap Lajoie

**QUESTION 138:** There have been six managers in franchise history to lead the club to the postseason. Three of the five Pennants in franchise history were claimed before the divisional play era—meaning the Pennant was won by claiming the league's best regular season record, and then you advanced straight to the World Series. Three of the six managers claimed a Pennant during that era. Three of the six made it to the postseason by virtue of winning a Division Title. Only one of the six, however, has this misfortune: he's the only postseason manager in franchise history to go winless in October. Who is the only Indians manager to guide the club to the postseason but not win a single game?

a) Charlie Manuel
b) Al Lopez
c) Tris Speaker
d) Eric Wedge

**QUESTION 139:** At a club's inception, winning a championship is the ultimate goal, but the first priority is to piece together a winning season. You read already that Cleveland was 54-82 during its inaugural season in the AL ... but do you know who was the first manager in franchise history to post a winning record for an entire season?
a) Jimmy McAleer
b) Bill Armour
c) Nap Lajoie
d) Deacon McGuire

**QUESTION 140:** Only one manager in franchise history has had to deal with this particular pressure: a one-game playoff to end the regular season with a berth in the postseason on the line. Who managed the Indians to a one-game playoff victory vs. the Boston Red Sox?
a) Lou Boudreau
b) Mike Hargrove
c) Eric Wedge
d) Tris Speaker

# 7 ANSWER KEY

___ **QUESTION 121:** D
___ **QUESTION 122:** A
___ **QUESTION 123:** D
___ **QUESTION 124:** B
___ **QUESTION 125:** B
___ **QUESTION 126:** A
___ **QUESTION 127:** B
___ **QUESTION 128:** A
___ **QUESTION 129:** A*
___ **QUESTION 130:** C

___ **QUESTION 131:** B
___ **QUESTION 132:** D
___ **QUESTION 133:** A
___ **QUESTION 134:** C
___ **QUESTION 135:** A
___ **QUESTION 136:** C
___ **QUESTION 137:** A
___ **QUESTION 138:** B*
___ **QUESTION 139:** B*
___ **QUESTION 140:** A*

**KEEP A RUNNING TALLY OF YOUR CORRECT ANSWERS!**

Number correct:     ___ / 20

Overall correct:     ___ / 140

#129 – Lopez managed the club for six seasons, winning one Pennant and finishing second a gut wrenching five times. His career record was 570-354, good for the highest winning percentage in franchise history: .617.

#138 – Ironically, refer back to #124 and #129 … Lopez won the Pennant easily, setting all sorts of records along the way, before getting swept in the World Series. He later won a second Pennant as manager of the Chicago White Sox, but lost the World Series to the Los Angeles Dodgers—although his White Sox did win two games in that series.

#139 – It didn't take long—Armour was the club's second manager and he took over for Cleveland's second season and promptly posted a winning record for three straight years from 1902-04.

#140 – In 1948, and after defeating the Boston Red Sox to make the postseason, the club went on to defeat the Boston Braves to win the World Series.

*"It was something everyone [in Cleveland] could share. I had a lady come up to me and tell me she was in labor, and she told the doctor she's not going to have the baby until the game was over ... and she waited."*
— Len Barker, 30 years after pitching a perfect game on May 15, 1981

# 8 THE FABULOUS FEATS

**THE CLEVELAND INDIANS**, as one of the American League's founding teams, have played nearly 17,500 games since 1901. That's a lot of baseball: nearly 1,800 players and approximately 160,000 innings and more than 4.2 million outs. As a franchise the Indians are closing in on 160,000 hits, 80,000 runs, and 12,000 home runs. All of which leads to an obvious point—there's no shortage of "fabulous feats" in franchise history as there have been plenty of opportunities for Indians players to do extraordinary things on the diamond.

In this chapter you'll be tested on 20 fabulous feats, but again, our reactions to these moments are the same that we give to the hitters and pitchers who we love to talk about—meaning a fabulous feat can inspire us, leave us in awe, or leave us scratching our heads. For example, if a player sets a Major League record for shortstops and then agrees to move to third base the following season, you might say "he's a team player." And then the following season, when he sets a new Major League record for third basemen, you might say, "wow, that guy is really something." Well, in Cleveland history that guy would be Terry Turner. He established a Major League record for shortstops with a .973 fielding percentage in 1911, and then the club asked him to move to third base—so in 1912, he established a Major League record for third basemen with a .970 fielding percentage. And he could hit, too. Turner's play was definitely inspirational.

The antithesis of Turner?

That'd be Indians shortstop John Gochnauer, who not only batted just .185 in 1903, but he also set a Major League record for shortstops with 98 errors ... which explains why in 1904 the Indians brought in a new shortstop, a guy by the name of Turner.

Sometimes are feats aren't so fabulous, they're just dubious—but either way, they're fun to talk about.

Our questions though are focused on the truly fabulous—feats that, out of the thousands of players and innings and outs have been done only a handful of times; feats that, when you consider all the players and innings and outs from every other MLB team, were done first, or best, or more often by a guy wearing an Indians uniform … those are what we're testing here, so read on and enjoy.


**QUESTION 141:** In a game that saw the Indians tie a franchise record by hitting eight home runs during an 18-6 blowout of the Seattle Mariners, this player claimed a franchise record all his own as the first catcher in franchise history to hit three homers in one game. He was 5 for 5 and his home runs came from both sides of the plate. So what did he do after that? He got a well-earned day off for the next game, of course—but then he promptly came off the bench and hit a pinch-homer. Who was the first catcher in franchise history with a three-homer game?
  a)   Andy Allanson
  b)   Alan Ashby
  c)   Sandy Martinez
  d)   Victor Martinez

**QUESTION 142:** It took 15 years of play in the American League before anyone managed this extraordinary feat: a pinch-hit grand slam. This Tribe member was the first to come off the bench in grand style, but he had a bit of help, as the ball skipped through a small hole in the fence and the outfielder was unable to retrieve it. Anyway, he got credit for the grand slam. Who hit the first pinch-hit grand slam in American League history?
  a)   Marty Kavanagh
  b)   Bill Wambsganss
  c)   Terry Turner
  d)   Ray Chapman

**QUESTION 143:** Among the numbers retired by the Indians franchise is one set aside specifically for "The Fans." Cleveland sold out every home game from June 1995 through April 2001, establishing a Major League record for consecutive home sellouts that was later eclipsed by the Boston Red Sox. It was truly remarkable—demand for Indians tickets was so great during this time that on three separate occasions all 81 home dates were sold out *before* Opening Day. Now *that's* a fabulous feat. What is the number retired in honor of the fans?

a) 445
b) 455
c) 465
d) 475

**QUESTION 144:** This player compiled about three week's worth of slugging stats all in one afternoon. In the first game of a doubleheader he homered in three consecutive at bats. He added a double in the second half of the twin bill and had tallied nine RBIs on the day by the time the Senators got their heads together and drilled him with a pitch to back him off the plate. So after getting hit by a pitch, naturally he homered for the fourth time that afternoon in his next at bat. For the day: five hits, four home runs, four runs, and 11 RBIs. Who hit four home runs in a doubleheader vs. the Washington Senators that day?

a) Earl Averill
b) Hal Trosky
c) Larry Doby
d) Al Rosen

**QUESTION 145:** On July 31, 1963, the Indians became just the second team in Major League history to hit four consecutive home runs. Woodie Held hit the first blast with two outs and the bases empty in the home half of the sixth inning, and Pedro Ramos, Tito Francona, and Larry Brown followed him. Which of the following statements about this fabulous feat is true?

a) Pedro Ramos was a pitcher
b) The blast by Pedro Ramos was his second of the game
c) The blast by Larry Brown was his first career HR
d) All of the above

**QUESTION 146:** This legendary player wasted no time making history—he hit a home run in his first career at bat, becoming the first-ever player in American League history to do so. Who is he?

a) Joe Jackson
b) Hal Trosky

    c)    Earl Averill
    d)    Joe Sewell

**QUESTION 147:** This legendary player was a switch-hitter who once hit a pinch-hit grand slam. Oh, and he was a pitcher—one of only five in more than a century of baseball's modern era to hit a pinch-hit grand slam. As it happens, he's also the only player in franchise history to record his 300th career victory while wearing an Indians uniform. Who is he?
    a)    Bob Feller
    b)    Bob Lemon
    c)    Early Wynn
    d)    Cy Young

**QUESTION 148:** This pitcher was among the first in the game to use a slider—and seems like he used it pretty effectively. He set a franchise record by winning 15 consecutive starts and his only loss that year came on the season's final day. Who set this extraordinary record?
    a)    Addie Joss
    b)    Wes Ferrell
    c)    Cal McLish
    d)    Johnny Allen

**QUESTION 149:** The Texas Rangers selected Len Barker in the third round of the 1973 draft, but unquestionably his best seasons were spent pitching for the Indians. In 1980, he won 19 games and led the league with 187 strikeouts—both career highs. In 1981, Cleveland hosted the All-Star Game and Barker was there to toss two scoreless innings, and then he went on to lead the league in strikeouts again. And of course his finest moment was on May 15, that same season. Barker achieved baseball immortality when he took the mound, struck out 11 batters, and retired all 27 men he faced. If only for a day, he was absolutely perfect. Against which team did "Large Lenny" pitch a perfect game on May 15, 1981?
    a)    New York Yankees
    b)    Baltimore Orioles
    c)    Milwaukee Brewers
    d)    Toronto Blue Jays

**QUESTION 150:** Joe Sewell played 1,903 Major League games but struck out only 114 times in 7,132 career at bats—an unbelievable record. He spent 11 seasons in Cleveland where he averaged .320 in 1,513 games and established two other extraordinary records with his ability to put the ball in play. In 1925, he struck out only four times despite 699 plate appearances in 155 games. And he also established the record for consecutive games played without striking out. What's the record number of games that Joe Sewell played between strikeouts?

    a)   115
    b)   120
    c)   125
    d)   130

**QUESTION 151:** This Indians pitcher tossed a no-hitter, a very fabulous feat without question. But lots of guys have tossed a no-no—far more spectacular to do something that no one else ever has, which is exactly what this guy did: he *hit* a Major League record 38 home runs as a pitcher. Which Cleveland pitcher *slugged* his way into the record books?

    a)   Mel Harder
    b)   Wes Ferrell
    c)   Mike Garcia
    d)   Willis Hudlin

**QUESTION 152:** Pitching a no-hitter or a perfect game is impressive, and so is belting four homers in a game—but as a fan you're more likely to witness either of those feats than you are to be on hand for an unassisted triple play. Neal Bell was playing shortstop for the Indians when he turned the first unassisted triple play in baseball's modern era on July 19, 1909—but from 1928-2007 there was a grand total of *six* unassisted triple plays in Major League baseball. So the fans that witnessed this infielder turn the trick for the Indians on May 12, 2008 saw history in the making. Lyle Overbay, who hit into the triple play for the Blue Jays, quipped afterwards, "Hey, I'm just trying to speed up the game." Who pulled off this fabulous feat for the Indians (and then famously flipped the ball to a spectator in the stands)?

a)  Ryan Garko
b)  Asdrubal Cabrera
c)  Jhonny Peralta
d)  Casey Blake

**QUESTION 153:** The Philadelphia Athletics beat Cleveland 18-17 on July 10, 1932, in a game that took eighteen innings to finish. It was a wild, crazy game—Philadelphia scored two in the first, Cleveland answered with three in the bottom of the first; Philadelphia scored two in the fourth, Cleveland answered with three in the bottom of the fourth; Philadelphia scored seven in the seventh, Cleveland answered with six in the bottom of the seventh. By the time the ninth inning rolled around, Cleveland led 14-13. Philadelphia scored two in the ninth to take the lead, 15-14. Then Cleveland scored in the ninth to tie the game 15-15 and send it to extra-innings. Philadelphia scored two in the sixteenth, and Cleveland tied it again. And then finally, Philadelphia scored the winning run in the eighteenth inning. All total the teams combined for 35 runs, 58 hits, and six errors. But out of all the chaos one player emerged with a Major League record—he accounted for nine of the Indians 33 base hits. Who was 9 for 11 at the plate for the Indians that day?
a)  Dick Porter
b)  Johnny Burnett
c)  Ed Morgan
d)  Bill Cissell

**QUESTION 154:** The game was entirely different before pitch counts began dictating nearly every decision about a team's pitching staff. Take this legendary Indians hurler for example: he once tossed four consecutive complete game shutouts, pitched seven and eight innings respectively in his next two starts, and then reeled off a string of eight complete games in his next nine starts—including three more shutouts. He was so dominant during that stretch that he even went ten innings for a 1-0 victory, giving up just six hits while establishing a franchise record with *19 strikeouts*. Who is this pitcher?
a)  Bob Feller
b)  Bob Lemon
c)  Sam McDowell
d)  Luis Tiant

**QUESTION 155:** This member of the Tribe made history during a 15-5 thrashing of the New York Yankees—a switch-hitter, he became the first player in Major League history to hit home runs from both sides of the plate *in the same inning*. Who did this extraordinary feat?
   a)   Eddie Murray
   b)   Roberto Alomar
   c)   Carlos Baerga
   d)   Victor Martinez

**QUESTION 156:** This slugger was the first Major League player in six decades to eclipse 160 RBIs in one season, and he did it for the Tribe. Who is he?
   a)   Manny Ramirez
   b)   Jim Thome
   c)   Albert Belle
   d)   Travis Hafner

**QUESTION 157:** This player had the crowd at Jacobs Field chanting his name even though he wasn't in the starting lineup. That's because he'd gone 4 for 5 the day before against the Boston Red Sox, including a grand slam and a solo shot, and eight total RBIs ... and then the following game returned to his usual spot on the bench, seeing as he was only a part-time player. It can be tough to find your swing when you're not in the lineup every day, yet somehow this player forced his way into the lineup after he batted 10 for 16 with four home runs and 13 RBIs "filling in" during one week. He even won AL Player of the Week honors, which is pretty hard to do as a platoon player. Asked about his role with the team, he replied, "All I can do is try my best when I'm in there. My goal is to make it a difficult decision for them to keep me out of the lineup." Who played his way into the lineup with a monstrous week and then batted .321 with 13 home runs for the Indians in 2006?
   a)   Ryan Garko
   b)   Andy Marte
   c)   Franklin Gutierrez
   d)   Ben Broussard

**QUESTION 158:** You just read about the pitcher who set a franchise record when he struck out 19 batters in a ten-inning complete game—but do you know who holds the franchise record for strikeouts without going into extra-innings? This player struck out 18 batters in a nine-inning complete game. Who is he?

a)   Bob Feller
b)   Bob Lemon
c)   Sam McDowell
d)   Luis Tiant

**QUESTION 159:** This slugger hit 36 home runs in only 106 games and set a franchise record with his .714 slugging percentage, one of the top 30 season efforts in baseball history. Who is he?

a)   Manny Ramirez
b)   Jim Thome
c)   Albert Belle
d)   Rocky Colavito

**QUESTION 160:** This member of the Tribe set a franchise record by reaching base 311 times in one season. And then three years later, he did it again. It's one of the highest season totals in MLB history as well. Who did this fabulous feat not once, but twice for the Indians?

a)   Joe Jackson
b)   Nap Lajoie
c)   Tris Speaker
d)   Hal Trosky

# 8 ANSWER KEY

| | |
|---|---|
| ___ **QUESTION 141:** D | ___ **QUESTION 151:** B |
| ___ **QUESTION 142:** A | ___ **QUESTION 152:** B |
| ___ **QUESTION 143:** B* | ___ **QUESTION 153:** B |
| ___ **QUESTION 144:** A | ___ **QUESTION 154:** D |
| ___ **QUESTION 145:** D* | ___ **QUESTION 155:** C |
| ___ **QUESTION 146:** C | ___ **QUESTION 156:** A |
| ___ **QUESTION 147:** C* | ___ **QUESTION 157:** D |
| ___ **QUESTION 148:** D | ___ **QUESTION 158:** A |
| ___ **QUESTION 149:** D | ___ **QUESTION 159:** C |
| ___ **QUESTION 150:** A | ___ **QUESTION 160:** C |

**KEEP A RUNNING TALLY OF YOUR CORRECT ANSWERS!**

Number correct:  ___ / 20

Overall correct:  ___ / 160

#143 – It's displayed as "455 The Fans" in honor of 455 consecutive home sellouts.

#145 – Ramos was in fact a pitcher who hit two homers in the game—with the second being a part of history—and Brown was a shortstop who made history with his first career home run.

#147 – Cy Young was pitching for the Indians when he won his historic 500th career game.

*"Finally, it's your team that sucks!"*
— Drew Carey, comedian and Cleveland native

# 9 THE TEAMS

**THE CLEVELAND INDIANS** have won five Pennants and two World Series titles during ten trips to the postseason. Not every team has lived up to expectations, but that's not a problem exclusive to the Tribe—it's true for every Major League franchise. And despite the long dry spell between championships, Cleveland's managed to field some great teams and accomplish some remarkable feats.

Let's take a look.

**QUESTION 161:** This club hit a franchise record 220 home runs on its way to becoming the first team in American League history to hit 200-plus home runs in three consecutive seasons. What year did the Indians accomplish this feat?
    a)  1995
    b)  1997
    c)  1999
    d)  2001

**QUESTION 162:** The 2001 Seattle Mariners were quite a team, winning 116 games and leading all AL clubs in batting average, earned run average, and fielding percentage—just call it the "Team Triple Crown." It's a pretty rare feat. In fact, prior to 2001, the last team to be the best in the league in all three categories was Cleveland. What year did the Indians achieve this rare trifecta?
    a)  1948
    b)  1952
    c)  1954
    d)  1995

**QUESTION 163:** Some teams underachieve, but others just plain run into bad luck. Take the 1950 club. The Indians record was 92-62 that season. In the National League, the Philadelphia Phillies won the

Pennant with a 91-63 record. But over in the AL, 92 wins were only good enough for fourth place. Not much you can do about that, and not much you can do about what happened to the 1918 club either. Cleveland lost the Pennant by 1.5 games, but because the season was shortened due to World War I, home and away games were out of balance among teams around the league. Cleveland had to play 11 more road games than the team that won the Pennant. Which team beat Cleveland by 1.5 games in the standings after the scheduling quirk gave them 11 more games at home?

    a)   New York Yankees
    b)   Washington Senators
    c)   Boston Red Sox
    d)   Chicago White Sox

**QUESTION 164:** Perhaps this next team did underachieve ... it's the only one in baseball history to boast three 20-game winners *and* the league home run champion *and* the league RBIs champion and still miss the postseason. What year did the Indians dominate the leader boards but come up short in the only stat that really matters (wins)?

    a)   1952
    b)   1956
    c)   1959
    d)   1968

**QUESTION 165:** The New York Yankees led the league in team batting and earned run average during consecutive seasons in 1957-58, a feat no other team in the league could replicate until this Tribe club came along. And even better, for the first time in franchise history, the Tribe also posted the best record in baseball in these back-to-back seasons. What years did the Tribe so thoroughly dominate?

    a)   1994-95
    b)   1995-96
    c)   1996-97
    d)   1997-98

**QUESTION 166:** The first night game in American League history was played on May 16, 1939, in a game the Indians won 8-3 in ten innings. Which team did the Tribe beat in this historic game?

a)    Philadelphia Athletics
b)    Washington Senators
c)    Chicago White Sox
d)    Boston Red Sox

**QUESTION 167:** Cleveland made history on May 5, 1999, when the club rallied from a 10-2 deficit to win a game by the final score of 20-11. After trailing by eight runs, they won by a margin of nine—easily the biggest turnaround in big league history. Ironically, the team Cleveland beat that day would blow a 10-2 lead again in 2005, and would again lose by the score of 20-11. Which team did the Tribe rally against so effectively?
a)    Seattle Mariners
b)    Kansas City Royals
c)    Baltimore Orioles
d)    Tampa Bay ~~Devil~~ Rays

**QUESTION 168:** The 1972 Indians reached a literal low point on offense, scoring a franchise worst 472 runs. Just over a quarter-century later the offense was slugging its way through opposing pitchers just fine, thank you very much. Led by Roberto Alomar with 138 runs, the Tribe boasted five players who topped the century mark in runs scored and set a franchise record by crossing the plate 1,009 times. What year was the offense so prolific?
a)    1998
b)    1999
c)    2000
d)    2001

**QUESTION 169:** This Tribe squad could hit with the best of them. It set two franchise records with nine players who batted .300 or better for the entire season and a team .308 batting average. What year did the Tribe hit for such a high average?
a)    1920
b)    1921
c)    1948
d)    1954

QUESTION 170: The same offense that scored a franchise low 472 runs in 1972 also set the futility standard for RBIs with 440. That's a far cry from the Indians offense that boasted a franchise record four players with 100-plus RBIs (combined they had *509 RBIs*). What year did the Indians set this franchise record?
- a)  1998
- b)  1999
- c)  2000
- d)  2001

QUESTION 171: The 1954 club set all sorts of records but perhaps its most amazing feat is that it never lost more than nine games in any one month. In fact, it lost more than seven games in a month only twice all season—and in August, it set a franchise record for most wins in a month. How many games did the Indians win in August 1954?
- a)  22
- b)  24
- c)  26
- d)  28

QUESTION 172: Surprisingly, the longest winning streak in franchise history doesn't belong to the 1954 club. The record is 13, and it's been done twice—first in 1942, and then again in what season?
- a)  1948
- b)  1951
- c)  1995
- d)  1996

Question 173: From Blues to Bronchos to Naps … which team was the first in franchise history to be called the Indians?
- a)  1912
- b)  1913
- c)  1914
- d)  1915

QUESTION 174: It's crazy to imagine this today, but Hall of Fame legend Lou Boudreau was only *24-years-old* when he took the reigns as player-manager for the Indians. What year was it when the Tribe made him skipper?

a)  1938
b)  1940
c)  1942
d)  1944

**QUESTION 175:** Omar Vizquel, Roberto Alomar, and Travis Fryman all won Gold Gloves for this club that set an American League record for fewest errors (72) and highest fielding percentage (.988). What year did the Tribe field so cleanly?

a)  1998
b)  1999
c)  2000
d)  2001

**QUESTION 176:** This Indians club was agonizingly close to a Pennant, but came up a game short. It was the same year that Bob Feller pitched a no-hitter on Opening Day. The same year that Feller won 27 games. And the same year that the Indians trailed the Tigers by two games in the standings with three left to play, all at home, all against Detroit, with Feller on the mound to open the series against Floyd Giebell, who was making just his second career start. So of course Giebell outpitched Feller, the Tigers won 2-0 to take the Pennant, and Giebell never won another game the rest of his life. What year did the Tribe lose the Pennant by a single gut-wrenching game to the Detroit Tigers?

a)  1938
b)  1939
c)  1940
d)  1941

**QUESTION 177:** Bill Veeck was legendary for his promotional stunts to get fans to attend games—and he wasn't beyond installing a movable fence in centerfield to adjust for visiting teams either. When he bought the club two of his investors were Bob Hope and Hall of Famer Hank Greenberg. What year did Veeck purchase the Indians?

a)  1944
b)  1946

c) 1948
d) 1950

**QUESTION 178:** General manager Frank Lane made his mark on the club by making several unpopular or unsuccessful trades. Among the guys he traded to other teams are Rocky Colavito, Roger Maris, Norm Cash, and ... manager Joe Gordon? Uh, yes. Lane and Detroit GM Bill DeWitt traded managers—Joe Gordon for Jimmy Dykes. Lane's tenure ended shortly thereafter, long before the damage he caused. What year did the Indians and Tigers trade managers during mid-season?
a) 1958
b) 1960
c) 1962
d) 1964

**QUESTION 179:** The Indians have won more than 8,800 games during 112 years of play in the American League. Against which AL opponent do the Indians have more wins than any other?
a) Baltimore Orioles
b) Boston Red Sox
c) Detroit Tigers
d) New York Yankees

**QUESTION 180:** The Indians have lost more than 8,500 games in that same span ... not bad, all things considered, but against which AL opponent do the Indians have more losses than any other?
a) Baltimore Orioles
b) Boston Red Sox
c) Detroit Tigers
d) New York Yankees

# 9 ANSWER KEY

___ **QUESTION 161:** B      ___ **QUESTION 171:** C
___ **QUESTION 162:** A      ___ **QUESTION 172:** B
___ **QUESTION 163:** C      ___ **QUESTION 173:** D
___ **QUESTION 164:** A      ___ **QUESTION 174:** C
___ **QUESTION 165:** B      ___ **QUESTION 175:** C
___ **QUESTION 166:** A      ___ **QUESTION 176:** C
___ **QUESTION 167:** D      ___ **QUESTION 177:** B
___ **QUESTION 168:** B      ___ **QUESTION 178:** B
___ **QUESTION 169:** B      ___ **QUESTION 179:** A
___ **QUESTION 170:** B      ___ **QUESTION 180:** D

**KEEP A RUNNING TALLY OF YOUR CORRECT ANSWERS!**

Number correct: ___ / 20

Overall correct: ___ / 180

*"Every day is a new opportunity. You can build on yesterday's success or put its failures behind and start over again. That's the way life is, with a new game every day, and that's the way baseball is."*
— Bob Feller, Hall of Fame legend

# 10 THE POSTSEASON

ONE OF MY UNCLES, growing up in South Carolina in the mid-1900s, at the age of seven began his lifelong passion for the Cleveland Indians when they played the NY Giants in the 1954 World Series. Since his family had no television at the time, he was fixated on the Series through radio. Like all Cleveland fans, he felt the great disappointment of the favored Indians being swept by the Giants in four games. Little did he know at the time that he probably chose the most challenging time period to place his baseball hopes on the Tribe as it would be 41 more years before he could again have the opportunity to pull for his team in a postseason game.

But, as possibly South Carolina's only Cleveland Indians fan during his early years, the faith was always present. His hopes were renewed for periods each year as his favorites Rocky Colavito, Max Alvis, Vic Davalillo, Luis Tiant, Sonny Siebert and others inspired him to believe the next World Series for the Indians was close at hand. I have no doubt he feels he is the one who first coined the phrase "just wait 'til next year." In the '60s he had heated sessions with Dodger fans as to who was the better pitcher, Sandy Koufax or "Sudden Sam" McDowell. Sure, Sandy had a better W-L record, but Sam had more strikeouts, a better fastball, and etc.

While another World Series title for the Tribe is still "right around the corner," the more recent decades have provided several postseason appearances, resulting in a number of thrills as well as some disappointments. Certainly, beating the Yankees, Red Sox, Mariners, and Orioles during postseason play in the '90s and 2000s is a major step up from going home at the end of the regular season for 41 straight years.

Who knows, maybe another Series shot is in the near future?

In the meantime, let's check out our knowledge on some facts about the Tribes postseason experiences.

QUESTION 181: The modern era World Series was first played in 1903. The ALCS had its beginning in 1969 and the ALDS was played in 1981 and again each year since 1995. Including all games played in the ALDS, the ALCS, and the World Series from 1920 to 2011, which franchise team has Cleveland faced the most in postseason play?

    a)   New York Yankees
    b)   Boston Red Sox
    c)   (Boston, Milwaukee, Atlanta) Braves
    d)   Baltimore Orioles

QUESTION 182: The meeting of the Indians and the NY Giants in the 1954 World Series featured the batting champions from the National League and the American League facing each other for just the third time in a World Series. The NL batting champion that year was Willie Mays, the centerfielder for the Giants, who batted .345 during the regular season. Who led the AL with a .341 average for the Indians?

    a)   Vic Wertz
    b)   Bobby Avila
    c)   Larry Doby
    d)   George Strickland

QUESTION 183: Tris Speaker was the player-manager for the Indians in the 1920 World Series against the Brooklyn Robins, playing centerfield and batting .320 in the series. Earlier in his career he played in two other World Series with what team?

    a)   Boston Red Sox
    b)   New York Giants
    c)   Brooklyn Robins
    d)   Philadelphia Athletics

QUESTION 184: During the 1948 World Series, the Tribe returned home with a 3 games to 1 lead to play Game 5 of the series in Municipal Stadium against the Boston Braves. Cleveland fans turned out for the game in great numbers, setting an all-time attendance record. How many people were in attendance in this record crowd?

    a)   71,342
    b)   75,899

c)   81,238
d)   86,288

QUESTION 185: When Cleveland played against the Atlanta Braves in the 1995 World Series, which Indian pitcher defeated Greg Maddux in Game 5 of the Series after losing to him in Game 1?
a)   Orel Hershiser
b)   Dennis Martinez
c)   Charles Nagy
d)   Paul Assenmacher

QUESTION 186: This Cleveland leadoff batter started Game 2 of the 1954 World Series with a home run on the game's first pitch. Who is he?
a)   Al Smith
b)   Bobby Avila
c)   Al Rosen
d)   Bill Glynn

QUESTION 187: Three Cleveland pitchers had starts in the four-game 1954 World Series. Two of these were both 23 game winners during the season, Bob Lemon and Early Wynn. The third starter was a big right-hander with 19 wins and five saves, nicknamed "The Bear." Who was he?
a)   Mike Garcia
b)   Hal Newhouser
c)   Don Mossi
d)   Ray Narleski

QUESTION 188: Cleveland's first world championship was in 1920 when the Indians beat the Brooklyn Robins (now the LA Dodgers) 5 games to 2 in the World Series. The fifth game of that series had several significant moments. Elmer Smith hit the first World Series grand slam and Jim Bagby Sr. hit the first home run ever by a pitcher in a World Series. Another memorable feat in the game involved Bill Wambsganss, the Indians second baseman. What was his remarkable accomplishment in this game?
a)   He hit four doubles
b)   He hit for the cycle

c)   He stole five bases

d)   He turned an unassisted triple play

**QUESTION 189:** Which one of the Indians postseason series lasted the maximum number of games and was not decided until the eleventh inning of the final game?

a)   1996 ALDS

b)   1948 World Series

c)   1998 ALCS

d)   1997 World Series

**QUESTION 190:** In the 1948 World Series, one pitcher won two of the Tribe's four victories, pitching a one-run complete Game 2 and seven strong innings of the 4-3 win in Game 6. Who is this pitcher?

a)   Bob Feller

b)   Bob Lemon

c)   Gene Bearden

d)   Steve Gromek

**QUESTION 191:** During Game 6 of the 1995 World Series vs. the Atlanta Braves, the Indians Kenny Lofton set a record for the most stolen bases in one World Series game. He stole how many bases in this game?

a)   3

b)   4

c)   5

d)   6

**QUESTION 192:** A Cleveland pitcher in a 1920 regular season game pitched seven full innings in a game before he threw a ball—*seven straight innings of all strikes.* In 1918, this same pitcher had pitched and won a 19-inning complete game against the NY Yankees at the Polo Grounds. In the 1920 World Series, he won all three games he pitched, with each of them being a 5-hit complete game. Who did these extraordinary feats?

a)   Stan Coveleski

b)   Jim Bagby Sr.

c)   Ray Caldwell

d)   George Ellison

**QUESTION 193:** The 1948 Indians qualified to play in the World Series by beating the Boston Red Sox in the first one-game AL Pennant playoff in history as both teams finished the regular season with a record of 97-58. Which Indian player hit two home runs in this game to propel his team into the World Series?

 a) Larry Doby
 b) Thurman Tucker
 c) Jim Hegan
 d) Lou Boudreau

**QUESTION 194:** A follow-up ... who was the rookie left-handed pitcher who defeated the Bosox in the 1948 playoff game?

 a) Russ Christopher
 b) Bob Muncrief
 c) Gene Bearden
 d) Ed Kileman

**QUESTION 195:** In the final game of the 1995 ALCS, Kenny Lofton scored from second base on a passed ball. This score was followed by a home run off Seattle pitcher Randy Johnson, which helped send the Tribe to the World Series for the first time since 1954. Who hit the home run?

 a) Jim Thome
 b) Carlos Baerga
 c) Albert Belle
 d) Tony Pena

**QUESTION 196:** There were five team members who played for the Indians in both the 1948 World Series and the 1954 Series. Which one of the following players did *not* play in both of these series?

 a) Larry Doby
 b) Bob Feller
 c) Jim Hegan
 d) Bob Lemon

**QUESTION 197:** The best regular season winning margin for the Cleveland franchise over the second place team going into postseason play was a whopping 30 games. This cakewalk into the postseason occurred in which year?

a)  1920
b)  1954
c)  1995
d)  1997

**QUESTION 198:** In 1997, Cleveland moved into the World Series against the Florida Marlins with a 1-0 victory in the twelfth inning of the sixth game of the ALCS on a home run by Tony Fernandez. Which team did the Indians beat in this ALCS?
a)  New York Yankees
b)  Boston Red Sox
c)  Baltimore Orioles
d)  Seattle Mariners

**QUESTION 199:** After decades of falling short in the annual AL Pennant chase, the Indians first postseason victory in 47 years occurred in the 1995 ALDS over the Boston Red Sox by means of a thirteenth-inning walkoff homer. Who hit the dramatic big fly?
a)  Eddie Murray
b)  Tony Pena
c)  Jim Thome
d)  Albert Belle

**QUESTION 200:** The pitching staff for the 1954 Indians was considered the best in the majors with the team winning an American League record 111 games. However, the Giants swept the Indians in four games in the World Series and one of the Tribe's best power pitchers suffered two surprising losses in the series. Who did the Giants beat twice on their way to victory in the World Series?
a)  Bob Lemon
b)  Early Wynn
c)  Mike Garcia
d)  Bob Feller

# 10 ANSWER KEY

| | |
|---|---|
| ____ **QUESTION 181:** B* | ____ **QUESTION 191:** D |
| ____ **QUESTION 182:** B | ____ **QUESTION 192:** A |
| ____ **QUESTION 183:** A | ____ **QUESTION 193:** D |
| ____ **QUESTION 184:** D | ____ **QUESTION 194:** C |
| ____ **QUESTION 185:** A | ____ **QUESTION 195:** B |
| ____ **QUESTION 186:** A | ____ **QUESTION 196:** B* |
| ____ **QUESTION 187:** A | ____ **QUESTION 197:** C |
| ____ **QUESTION 188:** D | ____ **QUESTION 198:** C |
| ____ **QUESTION 189:** D* | ____ **QUESTION 199:** B |
| ____ **QUESTION 190:** B | ____ **QUESTION 200:** A |

**KEEP A RUNNING TALLY OF YOUR CORRECT ANSWERS!**

Number correct:     ____ / 20

Overall correct:     ____ / 200

#181 – The Indians and Red Sox have done battle four times—three times in the ALDS and once in the ALCS, with the two teams splitting the four series, 2-2.

#189 – The Tribe led Game 7 vs. the Florida Marlins in the 1997 World Series until the ninth inning, but the Marlins scored a tying run in the bottom of the ninth, and then scored again for the win in the eleventh on an RBI single by the Fish's Edgar Renteria.

#196 – Bob Feller was on both the 1948 and 1954 Cleveland teams, but being near the end of his career, he did not pitch or play in the 1954 series.

# CLEVELAND INDIANS IQ

### 190-200
*Genius Indians IQ exceeds Bob Feller and Lou Boudreau*

### 180-189
*Genius Indians IQ destined to be a First Ballot Hall of Famer*

### 170-179
*Genius Indians IQ is worthy of a world championship*

### 160-169
*Superior Indians IQ is worthy of Legendary Status*

### 150-159
*Superior Indians IQ makes you one of the All-Time Greats*

### 140-149
*Outstanding Indians IQ that places you among the top players*

### 130-139
*Above average Indians IQ that earns you a nice paycheck*

### 120-129
*Solid Indians IQ that lets you play ball for a living*

### 110-119
*Average Indians IQ good enough to get you a cup of coffee*

### 100-109
*Average Indians IQ got you a year of rookie ball*

# ABOUT THE AUTHORS

**TUCKER ELLIOT** is a Georgia native and a diehard baseball fan. A former high school athletic director and varsity baseball coach, he now resides and writes fulltime in Tampa, FL.

**DERRYL WALDEN** is a lifelong baseball fan who lives in Cary, NC with his wife, Betty. When not writing, he enjoys travel and time with family.

# REFERENCES

**WEBSITES**
Baseball-reference.com
MLB.com (and the official team sites through MLB.com)
BaseballHallofFame.org
ESPN.com
SABR.org
Baseball-Almanac.com

**VIDEOS**
MLB Productions 1954 World Series Video (2001 MLB Properties, Inc.)

**BOOKS**
*Baseball, an Illustrated History,* Geoffrey C. Ward and Ken Burns
*The Team by Team Encyclopedia of Major League Baseball,* Dennis Purdy
*The Unofficial Guide to Baseball's Most Unusual Records,* Bob Mackin
*The 2005 ESPN Baseball Encyclopedia,* edited by Pete Palmer and Gary Gillette
*100 Years of the World Series,* Eric Enders
*Tales from the Tribe Dugout,* by Russell Schneider
*The Glory of Their Times,* by Lawrence S. Ritter

# ABOUT BLACK MESA

Look for these titles in the popular Trivia IQ Series:

- *Atlanta Braves*
- *New York Yankees*
- *Cincinnati Reds*
- *Tampa Bay Rays*
- *Washington Nationals*
- *Philadelphia Phillies*
- *Baltimore Orioles*
- *Boston Red Sox (Volumes (I & II)*
- *Milwaukee Brewers*
- *St. Louis Cardinals (Volumes I & II)*
- *Major League Baseball*
- *Mixed Martial Arts (Volumes I & II)*
- *Boston Celtics (Volumes I & II)*
- *University of Florida Gators Football*
- *University of Georgia Bulldogs Football*
- *University of Oklahoma Sooners Football*
- *University of Texas Longhorns Football*
- *Texas A&M Aggies Football*
- *West Point Football*
- *New England Patriots*
- *Buffalo Bills*
- *Kentucky Derby*
- *NHL*
- *Rock & Roll*
- *The Beatles*

Look for these titles in the Sports by the Numbers Series:

- *Major League Baseball*
- *New York Yankees*
- *Boston Red Sox*
- *San Francisco Giants*
- *Atlanta Braves*
- *Texas Rangers*
- *University of Oklahoma Football*
- *University of Georgia Football*
- *Penn State Football*
- *NASCAR*
- *Sacramento Kings Basketball*
- *Mixed Martial Arts*

For information about special discounts for bulk purchases or how to use our books for group fundraising efforts, please email:

www.blackmesabooks.com
black.mesa.publishing@gmail.com

*The following is an excerpt from*

# Cincinnati Reds IQ: The Ultimate Test of True Fandom

## TUCKER ELLIOT
## JOE SORIANO

*Available from Black Mesa Publishing*

# Introduction

I HAVE A Cincinnati Reds 1978 Yearbook Magazine that my dad paid $1.50 for at a Spring Training game in Tampa, FL. Pete Rose is on the cover with the caption "Pete Rose and the 3,000 Hit Club" and inside the magazine is an article on his quest to reach 3,000 hits (he began the season needing just 34 to become only the 13th player in history to reach that plateau). It also discusses his goal to become the National League's all-time hits leader ... no mention of the MLB record Rose would later eclipse.

On page 7 is a great picture of Tom Seaver—and lucky for me, mine is autographed. Same with the picture of Paul Moskau on page 13, George Foster on page 17, and Davey Concepción on page 25.

It's a great souvenir that brings back a lot of memories—and thanks to Spring Training, Cincinnati was my "first" team.

Later, my first regular season Major League game was Atlanta vs. Cincinnati and my favorite player, Johnny Bench, hit a grand slam.

After writing or collaborating on more than two dozen baseball history and trivia books, I'm glad I finally have the opportunity to write about and pay tribute to one of baseball's great franchises, and the one that helped instill my lifelong love for the game when I was just a kid.

Sparky Anderson wasn't just my favorite manager ... he was my *mom's* favorite manager.

And in our backyard wiffle ball games, my brothers and I stood at the plate and imitated the batting stances of Pete Rose, Joe Morgan, George Foster, Tony Pérez, and Johnny Bench.

We even practiced flapping our back elbows like Joe Morgan as we tried to imagine what it was like to be a two-time MVP, a World Series hero, and a two-time World Champion ... in back-to-back seasons.

We worked hard to be like the guys on the mound, too. Our favorite was Tom Seaver, of course. If you didn't hit dirt with your right knee when you shoved off the mound, well ... then you just didn't have what it took to be like Tom Terrific.

Later it was Mario Soto, and later still it was Jose Rijo ... but no matter what the year, the team was always the Cincinnati Reds. I hope this book brings back many great baseball memories for you, just as it did for me.

This is a book of history and trivia that covers all eras of Reds baseball—however, to honor the legacy of Sparky Anderson and the Big Red Machine, we have chosen to introduce each chapter of questions with a profile of one of the players from that extraordinary era ... but we'll begin with the man who led them: Sparky Anderson.

Now sit back, challenge yourself, and enjoy.

*Tucker Elliot*
*Tampa, FL*
*August 2011*

*"I got good players, stayed out of their way, let them win a lot, and then just hung around for 26 years."*
*— Sparky Anderson, Hall of Fame Induction Speech*

## Sparky Anderson

**WHEN SPARKY ANDERSON** began his tenure as Reds manager in 1970 his resume had a few glaring holes. Historically, success as a player at the big league level does not necessarily translate to success as a big league manager—in fact, the opposite is more often true. In the fall of 1969 and continuing through spring of 1970, however, Sparky Anderson's playing career (or lack thereof) was the opening argument diehard fans used when speaking out against the newly hired skipper.

It was an easy target, considering his big league career consisted of one year playing second base for the Phillies.

In 1959, Sparky batted just .218 in 152 games. Only 12 of his 104 big league hits went for extra bases ... and none of them left the yard. He was your typical scrappy middle infielder, slight in build but heavy in what he called "spit and vinegar." Sparky was relegated to Triple-A ball in 1960, again in 1961, again in 1962, and yet again in 1963.

In 1964, the 30-year-old ballplayer hung up his spikes after 11 professional seasons and decided to earn a living painting houses.

That argument alone was enough for many to rest the case against Sparky—but for others there was a much stronger and entirely valid point to be made against his hiring, and it was simply this: he'd never managed a big league team before. When General Manager Bob Howsam announced on October 9, 1969, that Sparky Anderson would take over as Reds skipper for 1970, papers all across Ohio ran this headline the following day: "Sparky Who?" Cincinnati had loads of talent ... but was it realistic to expect a rookie manager to lead the franchise?

Howsam thought so—in fact, he said of Sparky, "We had some very good players but they needed to know how to do certain things. We thought they needed work in fundamentals and Sparky was extremely capable of that."

Sparky's rise to the rank of big league manager had gone much quicker than his path to becoming a big league player—and his career as a manager would last 25 years longer and be infinitely more successful. After paying his dues as a minor league skipper from 1964 through 1968, Sparky joined the San Diego Padres coaching staff in 1969. And with one season as a major league coach under his belt, in 1970 he began his journey to the Hall of Fame as the manager of the Cincinnati Reds.

It took exactly one month of regular season play for fans to accept Sparky—posting a 16-6 record out of the gate has that kind of effect. The club won 20 more games in May, and by the time July 26 rolled around, Cincinnati beat St. Louis 12-5 in the season's 100th game as the Reds improved to 70-30 and increased their Division lead to 12.5 games.

The Reds were a more human 32-30 the rest of the way, but that was more than good enough to clinch a Division title by 14.5 games over the Los Angeles Dodgers. Sparky then led the Reds to a clean sweep of the Pittsburgh Pirates to claim the National League Pennant—and despite falling in five games to the Baltimore Orioles during the 1970 World Series, it was clear to anyone paying attention that Cincinnati was on the verge of something special.

His tenure with the club would last nine seasons and 1,450 regular season games and result in 863 wins—Bill McKechnie is the only other skipper to manage the Reds for as many seasons as Sparky, but no one has been at the helm for more games or wins.

There was, of course, a sophomore slump in 1971 that saw the Reds finish a disappointing fifth in the standings.

However, Cincinnati then reeled off four Division titles in five seasons—including back-to-back World Series titles in 1975 and 1976 that cemented the legacy of Sparky Anderson and The Big Red Machine. And for Sparky, who was elected to the Baseball Hall of Fame by the Veterans Committee in 2000, it is his legacy as the manager of the Big Red Machine that endures and has earned him a place among the game's truly elite skippers. Very few who manage a big league club are successful, fewer still are the ones who experience success over an extended period of time, but to achieve a level of success so extraordinary that it is given a category all it's own—"The Big Red Machine"—places Sparky in one of the most exclusive and elite clubs in baseball history.

## TOP OF THE FIRST

**QUESTION 1:** He managed the club for nine seasons and seven times won 90-plus games. He was also the manager of the Big Red Machine. Who is this legend and what is the number retired in his honor?

**QUESTION 2:** He was an All-Star shortstop who became the team captain in 1983. Who is this legend and what is the number retired in his honor?

**QUESTION 3:** Major League Baseball honors this former manager annually when an award that bears his name is given to a current ballplayer "who best exemplifies [his] character and fighting spirit." Who is this legend and what is the number retired in his honor? His number was the first in franchise history to be retired.

**QUESTION 4:** He was a ten-time All-Star, five-time Gold Glover, two-time league MVP, and two-time World Champion with the Big Red Machine. Who is this legend and what is the number retired in his honor?

**QUESTION 5:** Cincinnati's official website calls him "perhaps the greatest catcher to ever play in the major leagues." Who is this legend and what is the number retired in his honor?

**QUESTION 6:** The Reds' official website calls him "the heart and soul of Cincinnati's Big Red Machine." He was the third member of the Big Red Machine to be inducted into the Baseball Hall of Fame when he was enshrined on July 23, 2000. Who is this legend and what is the number retired in his honor?

**QUESTION 7:** He blasted 30-plus homers seven times during ten seasons (1956-65) with Cincinnati to begin his Hall of Fame career. Who is this legend and what is the number retired in his honor?

**QUESTION 8:** Cincinnati's official website says "he was noted as the greatest left handed slugger and one of the best fielding first basemen in club history." He hit 251 homers for the Reds from 1947-57. Who is this legend and what is the number retired in his honor?

**QUESTION 9:** This baseball icon is the only player to have his number retired by every major league team—including Cincinnati, although he never played for the Reds. Who is this legend and what is the number retired in his honor?

**QUESTION 10:** He's arguably the greatest baseball player not yet in the Hall of Fame—and so far (as of 2011) he's not even in the Cincinnati Reds Hall of Fame, but he's still a legend. Who is this legendary pariah and what jersey number did he wear for Cincinnati?

## TOP OF THE FIRST ANSWER KEY

\_\_\_ **QUESTION 1:** Sparky Anderson, #10
\_\_\_ **QUESTION 2:** Dave Concepción, #13
\_\_\_ **QUESTION 3:** Fred Hutchinson, #1
\_\_\_ **QUESTION 4:** Joe Morgan, #8
\_\_\_ **QUESTION 5:** Johnny Bench, #5
\_\_\_ **QUESTION 6:** Tony Pérez, #24
\_\_\_ **QUESTION 7:** Frank Robinson, #20
\_\_\_ **QUESTION 8:** Ted Kluszewski, #18
\_\_\_ **QUESTION 9:** Jackie Robinson, #42
\_\_\_ **QUESTION 10:** Pete Rose, #14

### KEEP A RUNNING TALLY OF YOUR CORRECT ANSWERS!

Number correct:          \_\_ / 10

Overall correct:          \_\_ / 10

## BOTTOM OF THE FIRST

**QUESTION 11:** Harry Dalton, a legendary baseball executive in his own right, said of this Reds legend, "Every time [he] throws, everybody in baseball drools." Who is the legend Dalton was referring to?

**QUESTION 12:** He spent six years playing second base for Cincinnati but he's in the Hall of Fame because of his managerial career in the Bronx. It was in New York where he won three World Championships, the first three in Yankees franchise history. Can you name the second baseman that became a managerial legend in the Bronx?

**QUESTION 13:** Fellow-Hall of Famer Billy Herman said of this Reds legend, "If he were playing today, on this artificial surface, I don't know where the infielders would play him. The ball comes off there like a rocket, and the way [he] hit it, he might kill an infielder today. He could hit a ball as hard as anybody I ever saw, and that includes Ruth and Foxx." Can you name the Hall of Fame catcher Herman was referring to?

**QUESTION 14:** In his Hall of Fame induction speech, this legend said, "I take my vote as a salute to the little guy, the one who doesn't hit 500 home runs. I was one of the guys that did all they could to win." Do you know which legend spoke those words?

**QUESTION 15:** This slugger once said, "Pitchers did me a favor when they knocked me down. It made me more determined. I wouldn't let that pitcher get me out. They say you can't hit if you're on your back, but I didn't hit on my back. I got up." And trust me, pitchers feared this legendary slugger. Can you name him?

**QUESTION 16:** Reggie Jackson once said of this pitching legend, "He's so good that blind people come to the park just to hear him pitch." Not exactly sure how tactful that statement was, but he really did say it. Who was Jackson referring to?

**QUESTION 17:** In Game 7 of the 1975 World Series, the Boston Red Sox led Cincinnati 3-0 during the sixth inning when this player hit a two-run homer to jumpstart the Reds offense. Bill Lee, who was pitching for Boston, said, "I had been having good success with [him], throwing him my slow, arching curveball, so I thought it would be a good idea to throw it to him again. Unfortunately, so did [he], who timed it beautifully. He counted the seams of the ball as it floated up to the plate, checked to see if Lee MacPhail's signature was on it, signed his own name to it, and then jumped all over it." Who homered against Lee to spark the Reds comeback vs. the Red Sox?

**QUESTION 18:** On August 26, 1939, Cincinnati met the Brooklyn Dodgers in the first game to be televised on live TV. The Dodgers won the game 6-1, but this Reds third baseman became the first player in baseball history to bat on live TV. Do you know his name?

**QUESTION 19:** He won his first career batting title with a .335 average in 1968. With that title, he also became the first switch-hitter in N.L. history to win a batting crown. Who is this switch-hitter?

**QUESTION 20:** This legendary Reds manager became the first skipper in baseball history to manage and lose the All-Star Game for both the National League and the American League. Can you name him?

## Bottom of the First Answer Key

___ **Question 11:** Johnny Bench
___ **Question 12:** Miller Huggins
___ **Question 13:** Ernie Lombardi
___ **Question 14:** Joe Morgan
___ **Question 15:** Frank Robinson
___ **Question 16:** Tom Seaver
___ **Question 17:** Tony Pérez
___ **Question 18:** Billy Werber
___ **Question 19:** Pete Rose
___ **Question 20:** Sparky Anderson

## Keep a Running Tally of Your Correct Answers!

Number correct:            ___ / 10

Overall correct:           ___ / 20

Made in the USA
Middletown, DE
16 July 2018